Common Tree Diseases
of British Columbia

Common Tree Diseases
of British Columbia

E. A. Allen, D. J. Morrison,
and G. W. Wallis

Natural Resources Canada
Canadian Forest Service

1996

Canadian Forest Service
Pacific Forestry Centre
506 West Burnside Road
Victoria, British Columbia
V8Z 1M5
Canada

Phone (250) 363-0600

www. pfc.cfs.nrcan.gc.ca

Printed in Canada

Second printing - March 1998
Third printing - September 2000

Canadian Cataloguing in Publication Data

Allen, Eric Andrew, 1955

Common tree diseases of British Columbia

Includes bibliographical references.
"This is the third version of a Canadian Forest Service
tree disease identification guide for British Columbia"-- Introd.
ISBN 0-662-24870-8
Cat. no. Fo42-257/1996E

1. Trees -- Diseases and pests -- British Columbia -- Identification.
2. Trees -- Wound and injuries -- British Columbia -- Identification.
I. Morrison, D.J.
II. Wallis, G.W.
III. Pacific Forestry Centre.
IV. Title.

SB605.C3A45 1996   634.9'6'09711   C96-980313-3

Contents

Acknowledgments

Many people have contributed to the development of this book. Special thanks are due to the technical reviewers: Brenda Callan, John Dennis, Rod Garbutt, Yasu Hiratsuka, Richard Hunt, Kathy Lewis, Ralph Nevill, Scott Redhead, Richard Reich, George Reynolds, Richard Robinson, Rona Sturrock, Jack Sutherland, Bart van der Kamp, Alan Van Sickle, and Ron Wall. Other assistance was provided by Andrew Fisher, Simon Franklin, Rena Last, Josefine and Tim Qureshi, Fiona Ring, Sherry M. Singh, Daryn Swanson, Alan Thompson, and Nicole Wallace. Technical production was guided by Jill Peterson, Steve Glover, Rob Keip, and Jennifer Adsett, with layout by Soren Henrich.

Financial support was provided by the Canada-British Columbia Partnership Agreement on Forest Resource Development (FRDA II), and by Forest Renewal B.C., a crown corporation committed to renewing the forest sector in British Columbia.

CANADA-BRITISH COLUMBIA
PARTNERSHIP AGREEMENT ON
FOREST RESOURCE DEVELOPMENT:
FRDA II

BC 🌿

How this book is organized

The diseases included in this book are organized according to type of disease (e.g., rusts, cankers, mistletoes) or the part of the tree that is affected (e.g., heart rots, root diseases). Within these groupings, diseases are identified by their common name, as recognized by the Western International Forest Disease Work Conference in 1984 (Hawksworth *et al.* 1985). The latin name of the disease-causing agent is listed, along with older names by which the organism was previously known. We have recognized the latin names and authorities in the American Phytopathological Society publication *Fungi on plants and plant products in the United States* (Farr *et al.*, 1989).

The list of hosts affected by a particular disease comes from two sources: the Canadian Forestry Service host-fungus index that lists fungi collected in British Columbia since 1889, and Farr *et al.* (1989), which lists hosts for other parts of North America. Where a disease occurs mainly on one host, but has also been reported on other hosts, the most important host(s) is printed in **bold-face type**. A listing of common and latin names of host plants follows the disease descriptions. Disease distributions were obtained from CFS Forest Insect and Disease Survey collection records (Infobase) or through personal communication with regional experts. The disease signs and symptoms that can be seen with the naked eye or with the aid of a low power (10×) hand lens are described. In addition, microscopic characteristics of the fungal fruiting bodies, spores, and fungal growth in culture are listed. Information included in this section was drawn from Nobles (1948), Ziller (1974), Stalpers (1978), Funk (1985), and Gilbertson and Ryvarden (1986, 1987). Important references are provided for each disease.

Following the disease descriptions are the common and latin names of all host plants listed in the descriptions. Also included is a glossary which defines scientific terms and less commonly used words. General references used extensively throughout the book are included in a separate section.

One of the most valuable sections in an identification guide is the index. Three indices are included in this book. The first, the host index, lists organisms that cause disease by host and affected plant part. Those listed in **bold-face** are those which we feel are the most common organisms for each host species. Hosts included in this index are restricted to the important commercial tree species in British Columbia.

The second index is a list of selected disease organisms grouped by distinctive signs or symptoms. This is valuable in narrowing down the causal agent when a prominent sign or symptom is present.

The final index, the general index, lists all diseases and disease-causing organisms by common name, genus, species, and where appropriate, previously used latin names.

Photo Credits

Eric Allen 2f, 3a, 3b, 3c, 3f, 3g, 3h, 3i, 3j, 3k, 4d, 5a, 5b, 5c, 5e, 6a, 6b, 6g, 6i, 7c, 8a, 8b, 9a, 9b, 9c, 9d, 9e, 9f, 10a, 10b, 11c, 11b, 12a, 12c, 13a, 14b, 14c, 15b, 17b, 18a, 18b, 19a, 19b, 19c, 20a, 20b, 20d, 20e, 20f, 21a, 21b, 21c, 23a, 23b, 24b, 24c, 24d, 24e, 25a, 28b, 28c, 28d, 28e, 29b, 31a, 31d, 31f, 32a, 32b, 32c, 32d, 32g, 34c, 34e, 34g, 34h, 35b, 35c, 36a, 37a, 37b, 37c, 37d, 39c, 39d, 39e, 40c, 42, 43a, 43b, 44b, 44c, 45a, 45b, 46a, 46b, 46c, 47a, 47b, 47c, 48a, 48b, 49a, 49c, 51a, 51b, 51c, 52b, 53a, 53b, 53d, 53e, 57b, 59a, 59b, 61c, 62e, 62h, 63c, 63g, 63h, 63i, 64a, 64b, 64k,

Gerry Allen 38a,

Pete Angwin 6e,

Rollie Banyard 15d, 25c

Joe Baranyay 63k,

Jack Bier 16c,

J.E. (Ted) Browne 15c,

Don Buckland 24a, 27a,

Brenda Callan 3l, 3m, 40b, 60c, 62c, 62d, 62f, 62i,

CFS 2a, 2g, 6d, 6f, 26a, 34a, 35f, 58d, 60d, 62g, 64c,

Ed Chatelle 36b, 36d,

Fern Corkum 16d,

Alex Craigmyle 55d,

John Dennis 14a, 30a, 30e,

Blake Dickens 26b,

Bob Erickson 11a, 31c, 31e, 35a, 36c, 36e, 50a, 51d, 53c, 54c, 56a, 57a, 60b, 61a, 61b, 63d, 64e, 64g, 64i, 64j,

Bob Ferris 64h,

FIDS 28f, 29c, 43c, 45d, 57d, 58b, 63b, 64l,

Shane Ford 31b,

Ray Foster 16e, 17c, 27b,

Al Funk 22, 41, 48c, 62a, 62b, 62j,

Rod Garbutt 7a, 7b, 40a, 54b,

Brian Geils 32f,

Yasu Hiratsuka 35e,

John Hopkins 39b, 50b, 54d, 56b, 56c, 63j, 51e,

Nick Humphries 33b, 45c,

Al Johnson 6c, 13b,

Peter Koot 4b, 34b, 54a, 61d, 63e,

David Lai 31g, 32h, 33c, 34d, 34f, 35d, 37e, 37f,

Bill McNaughton 25b

Bill Merilees 33a

Duncan Morrison 1a, 1b, 1c, 1d, 1e, 1f, 1h, 1i, 1j, 1k, 1l, 2b, 2c, 2d, 4a, 4c, 5d, 6h, 6j, 20c, 44a,

Alex Porter 17a,

Libby Fox 16a,

Richard Reich 3d, 3e, 32e, 33d,

Richard Robinson 18c, 49b,

Alan Stewart 15a, 28a, 63f,

Rona Sturrock 1g,

Jack Sutherland 30b, 30c, 30d, 30f,

Rod Turnquist 12b,

Leo Unger 52a, 55a, 55b, 55c, 56d, 58a, 58c, 64d,

John Vallentgoed 29a, 57c, 64f,

Cam Wilson 2e,

Colin Wood 39a,

Wolf Ziller 38b, 38c, 60a, 63a,

Introduction

This is the third version of a Canadian Forest Service tree disease identification guide for British Columbia. The first, *Some common tree diseases of British Columbia*, by J. E. Bier, was published in 1949. The next edition, *Common tree diseases of British Columbia*, by R. E. Foster and G. W. Wallis, was published in 1969 and reprinted in 1974. Since the second edition there have been many changes in the scientific names of the disease organisms and in the economic importance of hosts and diseases. This edition has been updated to provide new information, with more colour photographs, to aid in the identification of tree diseases common on the major commercial tree species in British Columbia. Although the book is primarily aimed at forestry professionals, it will also be useful for arborists, horticulturists, and homeowners as a guide in the diagnosis of disease on a wide range of plants.

Forest diseases, as described in this book, are injurious conditions, often expressed by the abnormal growth or development of trees and caused by agents other than fire or insects. Thus, diseases include disorders that reduce growth, lower wood quality, cause predisposition to attack by other agents, or culminate in the death of the trees. Diseased trees may be detected from symptoms or signs or both. Symptoms are expressed by a loss in health or abnormal development of a tree or its parts (e.g., unnatural colour changes, swellings, dwarfing, or wilting). Signs identify the causal agent of the disease (e.g., the fruiting body of a fungus or aerial parts of dwarf mistletoe plants).

Non-infectious or physiological diseases are caused by non-living agents and encompass a wide range of disturbances to the normal functioning of a tree (e.g., unusually high or low temperatures, excess or deficiency of water or nutrients, or pollution). Susceptibility to damage varies with the species, age, and vigour of the trees. Factors inducing physiological disorders may operate for only a brief period as in the case of frost, may extend over part of a growing season as in the case of prolonged drought, or their effect may be cumulative over a number of years as in the case of some pollutants.

Infectious diseases are caused by living agents such as fungi, bacteria, viruses, and higher plants, which attack trees to obtain nutrients essential to their development. The most important infectious diseases occurring in British Columbia are caused by fungi and dwarf mistletoes. The magnitude of damage depends on the relative susceptibility of the tree (host), the virulence of the causal agent and its life history, and the environmental and other circumstances that influence the resistance of the host and the growth and reproductive ability of the causal agent. Consequently, a disease may vary in importance among tree species in one region or in the same tree species in adjacent regions.

Infectious forest diseases are classified as native or introduced. Native diseases do not usually threaten the existence of a tree species, but some may cause severe losses in some stands. Introduced (extra-regional or foreign) diseases, such as white pine blister rust, may become epidemic and threaten the existence of a susceptible tree species throughout its entire range.

Microscopic examination is required to identify many causal agents of diseases, but most of those included in this handbook may be recognized by their symptoms or signs.

Armillaria Root Disease

Armillaria ostoyae (Romagnesi) Herink
(= *Armillaria obscura* Schaeff.:Fr.)

Armillaria sinapina (Bérubé & Dessureault)
(= NABS V) (NABS stands for "North American Biological Species")

Armillaria gallica Marxmüller & Romagnesi
(= *Armillaria bulbosa* (Barla) Kile and Watling; = NABS VII)

Armillaria cepistipes Velanovsky
(= NABS XI)

Armillaria nabsnona Volk & Burdsall
(= NABS IX)

Basidiomycotina, Agaricales, Tricholomataceae

The term "Armillaria root disease" refers to a group of diseases caused by several related *Armillaria* species, sometimes known as the Armillaria root disease complex. In some older literature the name *Armillaria mellea* (Vahl:Fr) P. Kumm. was used in a broad sense for all species in the group. Recent research has clarified the taxonomy of the fungi involved, identifying those that are commonly found in B.C. In this treatment of Armillaria root disease, *Armillaria ostoyae* will be discussed separately from the other species found in the province as it has the greatest impact on the management of coniferous trees.

Armillaria ostoyae

Hosts: In B.C., *Armillaria ostoyae* has been reported on amabilis, grand, and subalpine fir, European, Japanese, and western larch, Engelmann, Norway, Sitka, and white spruce, lodgepole, western white, mugo, bishop, Austrian black, maritime, ponderosa, Monterey, red, and Scots pine, Douglas-fir, western redcedar, western hemlock, western yew, rocky mountain juniper, Port Orford cedar, and Oregon boxwood. Host records specifically for *A. ostoyae* in other parts of North America are not available, but in these areas as well as in B.C. the fungus is likely found on a wide range of broadleaved trees, shrubs, and herbaceous plants.

Distribution: Circumpolar in the northern hemisphere and 49° to approximately 52-53°N in B.C.

Identification: On conifers, *A. ostoyae* causes crown symptoms typical of root diseases; that is, reduced leader growth and foliage discoloration and thinning (Fig. 1a). On trees where the fungus is present at the root collar, resin exudes through the bark of the lower bole (Fig. 1b). This symptom is most obvious on resinous tree species such as Douglas-fir and lodgepole pine, but rare on non-resinous species such as western redcedar. Among resinous species, it is more obvious on moist sites than dry sites. White mycelial fans occur in the bark and in the cambial zone under bark showing resinosis (Figs. 1c, 1d, 1e). On diseased trees and those that have been dead for several years, impressions of mycelial fans may be seen on the inner bark. In conifer stands, trees with cone-shaped basal lesions caused by *A. ostoyae* that have callus at the margin are common. On western redcedar, basal lesions are commonly covered with loose, dead bark and form a flattened face on the side of the tree bearing the lesion. Broadleaved trees and shrubs show reduced growth and sparse foliage before death, and red to brown foliage and mycelial fans at the base of the stem after death.

Figure 1a: Reduced leader growth and chlorotic foliage on *Armillaria* infected Douglas-fir.

Figure 1b: Resinosus on the lower stem of an *Armillaria* infected tree.

Figure 1c, 1d, 1e: *Armillaria* mycelial fans beneath bark of lower stems (1c), and roots (1d, 1e).

Dead and diseased trees usually occur in "disease centers," which appear as openings in the canopy, and may be as large as 0.1 ha in mature stands (Fig. 1f). However, in some stands, distinct centers are absent and diseased trees are scattered throughout the stand. In young plantations and natural stands, diseased trees occur around colonized stumps of the previous stand (Fig. 1g).

The fruiting bodies of *A. ostoyae* are cream to brown-coloured mushrooms with a 5-10 cm wide cap and a distinct ring on the stem (Figs. 1h, 1i). The mushrooms are produced from late summer to mid-autumn around the base of infected, living trees, killed trees, and colonized stumps. Fruiting bodies are also commonly growing from dead wood associated with scars on living trees. The incipient decay of *A. ostoyae* in roots on coniferous and broadleaved trees is yellow to brown in colour with a watersoaked appearance (Fig. 1j). Later, the decayed wood becomes stringy, gelatinous, and very wet.

Damage: *Armillaria ostoyae* causes growth loss and small amounts of butt rot in diseased trees, however mortality is the greatest cause of loss. The fungus can kill conifers in plantations and natural stands throughout a rotation when roots of healthy trees grow into contact with, or form root grafts with the roots of diseased trees (Fig. 1k). On the coast, *A. ostoyae* is seldom serious in trees older than about 15 years whereas in the interior, trees of all ages are killed.

Remarks: On sites infested by *A. ostoyae*, there are currently two management strategies that can be applied at the time of harvest to reduce losses in the next rotation: 1) reduce the amount of inoculum by removing stumps (Fig. 1l), and 2) regenerate the site with one or more resistant or poor-host species.

Other *Armillaria* species:

Armillaria sinapina (= NABS V) *Armillaria cepistipes* (= NABS XI)
Armillaria gallica (= NABS VII) *Armillaria nabsnona* (= NABS IX)

Hosts: The *Armillaria* species listed above have been found on living broadleaved trees and as saprophytes on stumps of these trees after felling. Occasionally, *A. sinapina* has been found on stumps of conifers. These *Armillaria* species are weakly pathogenic on living broadleaved trees and do not kill healthy conifers.

Distribution:
Armillaria sinapina: 49°N to approximately 57°N (widespread and common).
Armillaria gallica: southern Vancouver Island (Garry oak habitat)
Armillaria cepistipes: collections from Hope and Stewart, B.C.
Armillaria nabsnona: coastal and southwestern B.C.

Identification: Of the above-listed species only *A. sinapina* and *A. nabsnona* (the latter only in SW B.C.) will be encountered in commercial coniferous forests. The ranges of *A. ostoyae* and *A. sinapina* overlap south of approximately 52-53°N in B.C. It is difficult to distinguish between *A. ostoyae* and *A. sinapina* in a colonized stump because both produce white mycelial fans in the bark and cambial zone. However, *A. sinapina* produces an extensive network of monopodially-branched rhizomorphs while *A. ostoyae* produces small amounts of dichotomously-branched ones. In addition, the sporophores of *A. sinapina* are usually darker in colour, smaller, and more numerous than those of *A. ostoyae*.

Figure 1f: *Armillaria* root disease center in a 80- to 100-year-old Douglas-fir stand (30 years after partial cutting). Figure 1g: *Armillaria* fruiting bodies around a diseased Douglas-fir stump. Figures 1h, 1i: Fruiting bodies of *Armillaria ostoyae* associated with western larch (1h) and Douglas-fir (1i).

On broadleaved trees where the disease is advanced, top growth and the number and size of leaves may be reduced, particularly when the trees are stressed by other predisposing agents. Decay is white to yellow in colour and has a watersoaked appearance.

In mixed coniferous/broadleaved stands, the presence of diseased conifers indicates that *A. ostoyae* is present, whereas colonized stumps or diseased broadleaved trees suggests *A. sinapina* but does not exclude *A. ostoyae*.

Damage: The damage caused by these weakly pathogenic *Armillaria* species on broadleaved trees is minor. The fungi appear to spread slowly in diseased trees that are often stressed by another agent. Where *A. ostoyae* and a weakly pathogenic species occur together in a managed commercial forest, the latter may reduce the damage caused by *A. ostoyae* by colonizing root systems, thereby denying them to *A. ostoyae*.

Remarks: Damage that may be caused by weakly-pathogenic *Armillaria* species can be reduced by maintaining a high level of tree vigour. In urban situations where broadleaved trees are damaged or killed, they should be replaced by a suitable conifer species.

Microscopic Characteristics: Basidiospores hyaline, dextrinoid, weakly cyanophilic, thin to moderately thick-walled, smooth or slightly verruculose or rugulose with broad, blunt usually prominent apiculus, lacking germ pore. Spore print white to cream colour, darkening on drying and in herbarium material. Growth in culture slow, mat cream-yellow or brown, hyphae simple septate, some with characteristic minute hairlike projections on side walls, laccase positive. Rhizomorphs present in older cultures. Nobles (1965): 2 6 10 16 20 32 37 39 47 54 55 (code for *A. mellea*).

References:

Morrison, D. J., D. Chu, and A. L. S. Johnson. 1985. Species of *Armillaria* in British Columbia. Can. J. Plant Pathol. 7:242-246.

Morrison, D. J., G. W. Wallis, and L. C. Weir. 1988. Control of Armillaria and Phellinus root diseases: 20-year results from the Skimikin stump removal experiment. Can. For. Serv., Rep. No. BC-X-302.

Morrison, D., H. Merler, and D. Norris. 1992. Detection, recognition, and the management of Armillaria and Phellinus root diseases in the southern interior of British Columbia. Can. For. Serv., B.C. Min. For., FRDA Rep. No. 179.

Shaw, C. G. III and G. A. Kile. 1991. Armillaria Root Disease. USDA For. Serv. Agric. Hdbk. No. 691.

Figure 1j: Butt rot in Engelmann spruce. 1k: Transfer of *A. ostoyae* from a colonized stump to a living tree in a spaced stand. Figure 1l: Stump removal to reduce *Armillaria* inoculum.

Annosus Root and Butt Rot

Heterobasidion annosum (Fr.:Fr.) Bref.

(= *Fomes annosus* (Fr.:Fr.) Cooke)

(anamorph = *Spiniger meineckellum* (A. Olson) Stalpers)

Basidiomycotina, Aphyllophorales, Polyporaceae

Hosts: *Heterobasidion annosum* has a very wide host range including both coniferous and broadleaved species. It has been reported in B.C. on amabilis and grand fir, white and Sitka spruce, lodgepole pine, Douglas-fir, western redcedar, **western hemlock**, bigleaf maple, and alder. In other parts of North America it has also been found on mountain hemlock, California incense cedar, juniper, subalpine fir, western larch, ponderosa and western white pine, Engelmann spruce, chestnut, hickory, honeysuckle, apple, poplar, oak, sagebrush, *Arbutus*, *Arctostaphylos*, *Camellia*, *Cercocarpus*, *Chamaecyparis thyoides*, *Diospyros*, *Kalmia*, *Pachistima*, *Prunus* spp., antelope-brush, *Rhododendron*, *Sequoia*, and *Sequoiadendron*. Two forms of the fungus are recognized in North America: the p-type, which occurs mainly on pine, incense cedar, hardwood and brush, and the s-type, which infects other conifer species. The p-type will infect both p-and s-type hosts, whereas the s-type is restricted to s-type hosts. To date only the s-type has been detected in B.C.

Distribution: This fungus affects trees west of the coast mountains and in the ICH biogeoclimatic zone.

Identification: Fruiting bodies are perennial, woody to leathery, and vary in form from effused-reflexed or resupinate to bracket-like (Figs. 2a, 2b). The upper surface is zoned, dark brown to black, and has an acute margin. The lower surface is white to cream, and poroid; the pores are small and irregular in outline. The context is white to cream. Fruiting bodies are most often found on the underside of decayed roots of living and standing-dead trees. On standing trees, it may be necessary to remove the duff from around the root collar to locate them. Fruiting bodies may also be found on the underside of stems and/or roots of windthrown trees.

The incipient stage of *H. annosum* decay is a yellow-brown to red-brown stain (Fig. 2c), while in advanced stages the wood is reduced to a white stringy or spongy mass (Fig. 2d) containing numerous small black flecks running parallel to the grain. In the final stage, the wood is completely degraded, leaving a hollow butt. Decay may extend as high as 10-15 m in the stem (Fig. 2e). Small (2-4 mm diameter), cream-coloured mycelial pustules are frequently present on the surface of roots decayed by *H. annosum*. A useful diagnostic procedure to identify decay of *H. annosum* is to wrap an infected wood sample in moist paper, enclose it in a plastic bag, and store it at room temperature. Within 5-6 days, asexual fruiting structures (conidiophores) will form on the wood surface (Fig. 2f). When viewed with a hand-lens or dissecting microscope these have a characteristic hemispherical shape.

Figures 2a, 2b: Mature *Heterobasidion annosum* fruiting bodies.
Figure 2c: Incipient decay of *H. annosum* in western hemlock stump.
Figure 2d: White stringy decayed wood showing black flecks parallel to grain.

Microscopic Characteristics: Contextual generative hyphae thin-walled, simple septate. Growth in culture rapid, mat white with patches of yellow and buff, simple septae or rare clamp connections on large diameter hyphae, conidiophores with globose heads, laccase positive. Stalpers: 1 (2) 3 (6) (7) (8) (9) (11) (12) (13) (14) (15) 18 (19) 21 (22) (24) 25 (26) 30 31 (35) (38) (39) (40) 45 (48) (50) (51) 52 53 54 (55) (57) (64) (67) (80) (82) 83 86 87 (89) (90).

Damage: Trees younger than 15 years that have a major portion of their root system killed by *H. annosum* exhibit crown symptoms typical of other root diseases (i.e., reduction in leader and branch growth, chlorotic foliage, and a distress cone crop). In more mature trees, however, the fungus causes a butt rot and external symptoms are not readily discernible. Trees with extensive decay in the structural roots are subject to windthrow (Fig. 2g), and groups of windthrown trees may indicate the presence of pockets of annosus root rot.

Remarks: Spores are present in the atmosphere on the coast throughout the year and can be carried by air currents for many miles. Infection by spores occurs through wounds on stems or roots, or through cut surfaces of fresh stumps. The fungus moves to surrounding trees through root grafts or root contact. Stand thinning treatments or damage to trees from logging operations can therefore intensify annosus root rot problems. *Heterobasidion annosum* is able to survive in stumps for several decades. The treatment of stump surfaces with borax has been used to prevent spore infection. Other control recommendations include shortened rotations and avoidance of wounding during logging. Immature fruiting bodies of this fungus could be confused with *Fomitopsis pinicola* but can generally be distinguished by the location on the tree. In addition, *F. pinicola* has very regular pores (pin-hole like) whereas the pores of *H. annosum* are irregular in shape.

References:

Morrison, D. J. and A. L. S. Johnson. 1978. Stump colonization and spread of *Fomes annosus* 5 years after thinning. Can. J. For. Res. 8:177-180.

Otrosina, W. J. and R. F. Scharpf (tech. coord.). 1989. Proc. Symp. on research and management of annosus root disease (*Heterobasidion annosum)* in western North America. USDA For. Serv., Gen. Tech. Rep. PSW 116.

Figure 2e: Incipient butt rot in red alder stem.
Figures 2f: Conidia of *Heterobasidion annosum*.
Figure 2g: Windthrown western hemlock with annosus root rot.

Tomentosus Root Rot

Inonotus tomentosus (Fr.:Fr.) S. Teng.

(= *Polyporus tomentosus* (Fr.:Fr.))
(= *Onnia tomentosa* (Fr.) P. Karst.)

Basidiomycotina, Aphyllophorales, Polyporaceae

Hosts: *Inonotus tomentosus* has been reported in B.C. on amabilis and subalpine fir, **Engelmann, black,** and **white spruce,** lodgepole, ponderosa, and white bark pine, Douglas-fir, western hemlock, and western larch. In other parts of North America it has also been found on grand fir, western larch, western white pine, Sitka spruce, and western redcedar.

Distribution: *Inonotus tomentosus* is found most frequently in the spruce-pine forests in central and northern British Columbia, and at higher elevations in southern B.C.

Identification: Advanced root infection by *I. tomentosus* can often be recognized by reduced leader and branch growth, thinning of the foliage (Figs. 3a, 3b), stress cone crops, and death of the tree. Although rare, cankers and resinosis may be present at the base of stems and near the root collar. Wind-thrown trees or groups of dead and dying trees may indicate the presence of the disease in a stand. Fruiting bodies of *I. tomentosus* are small, usually less than 10 cm in diameter, stalked, and are found on the ground around infected trees (Fig. 3c). Similar, shelf-like fruiting bodies are also found on dead roots and at the base of infected stems (Fig. 3d), but these are generally produced only by a related species, *I. circinatus.* Fruiting bodies are annual and leathery, most commonly developing in August and September. The upper surface is yellow-brown to rust-brown and velvety. The whole fruiting body becomes dark brown with age.

The early stage of the decay is characterized by a red-brown discoloration in the heartwood (Fig. 3e). The advanced decay has large, elongated to rectangular spindle-shaped pits, separated by red-brown firm wood (Figs. 3f, 3g, 3h). The cross section of an infected stem has a honeycomb appearance. Stump surfaces often demonstrate these stages of decay and can be used to identify the presence of the disease (Figs. 3i, 3j, 3k).

Microscopic Characteristics: Contextual hyphae simple septate. Basidiospores hyaline, negative in Melzer's reagent, acyanophilous, smooth, ellipsoid, 5-6 × 3-4 µm. Setae are abundant, 7-11 × 50-70 (140) µm, straight (Fig. 3l) (compared to *I. circinatus,* which has hooked setae, Fig. 3m). Growth in culture slow, mat yellow-brown to brown, laccase positive. Stalpers: 1 3 4 (9) (11) (14) (15) 17 (18) 24 25 (26) 28 (30) (31) 34 (35) 38 48 52 53 (54) 64 67 80 [89] 90.

Figure 3a: Healthy (right) and *Inonotus tomentosus*-infected (left) spruce. The diseased tree shows reduced growth and a distress-crop of cones. Figure 3b: Crown symptoms in mature diseased spruce. Figure 3c: Fruiting bodies of *I tomentosus*. Figure 3d: Fruiting bodies of *I. circinatus*. Figure 3e: Heartwood discoloration in an infected root. Figure 3f: White pocket rot symptoms. Figure 3g: Honeycomb appearance of an infected root.

Damage: Infected trees may appear healthy but have extensive butt cull and reduced annual increment growth. The fungus spreads from tree to tree at points of root contact; consequently, diseased trees occur in groups and mortality results in "stand openings." Windthrow may occur before the death of an infected tree. Fruiting bodies on or around a tree indicate that three or more metres of rot may be present in the base of the stem. *Inonotus tomentosus* is a serious problem in second-growth stands as the stumps of infected trees provide an inoculum source for young trees.

Remarks: Two similar species of *Inonotus* are found in B.C., *I. tomentosus* and *I. circinatus*, which is thought to be less virulent. It is difficult to differentiate between the two, particularly when basidiocarps are not present. Basidiocarps of *I. tomentosus* are smaller and thinner and are usually form in groups whereas those of *I. circinatus* are larger, thicker, and tend to be found singly. *Inonotus circinatus* is less commonly found on spruce than *I. tomentosus*. Setal characteristics are a good diagnostic feature. The advances stages of decay may also be confused with that of *Phellinus pini*.

References:

Hunt, R. S. and L. Unger. 1994. Tomentosus root disease. Can. For. Serv., Forest Pest Leaf. No. 77. Victoria, B.C.

Whitney, R. D. 1977. *Polyporus tomentosus* root rot of conifers. Can. For. Serv. For. Tech. Rep. No. 18.

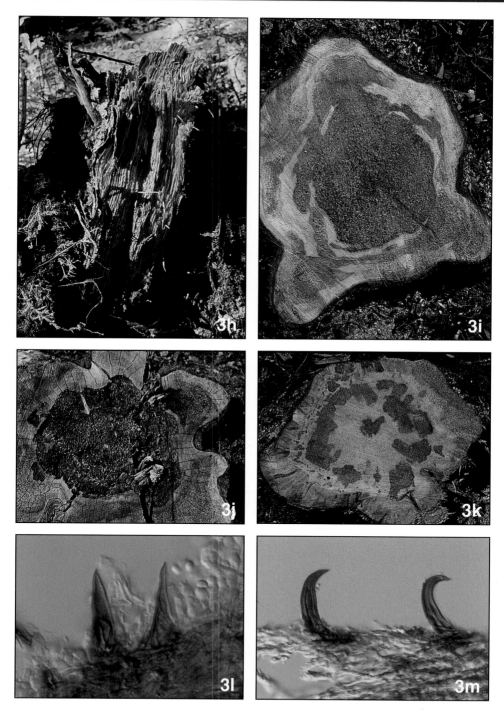

Figure 3h: Honeycomb appearance of an infected root.
Figures 3i, 3j, 3k: Decay evident in cross-sections of *Inonotus tomentosus*-infected spruce stumps.
Figures 3l, 3m: Setal hyphae of *I. tomentosus* (3l) and *I. circinatus* (3m).

Black Stain Root Disease

Leptographium wageneri (Kendrick) M. J. Wingfield
(= *Verticicladiella wageneri* (Kendrick))
(teleomorph = *Ophiostoma wageneri* (Goheen & Cobb) Harrington)

Deuteromycotina, Stilbellales, Stilbellaceae

Hosts: *Leptographium wageneri* has been reported in B.C. on Douglas-fir, lodgepole pine, western white pine, Engelmann and white spruce, and western hemlock. In other parts of North America it has also been found on mountain hemlock, ponderosa pine, and grand and white fir. In B.C., two varieties of the fungus are recognized based on host associations: *Leptographium wageneri* var *ponderosum* on pines and spruce, and *Leptographium wageneri* var *pseudotsugae* on Douglas-fir.

Distribution: Since the first report of black stain root disease in B.C. in 1976, this problem has been reported from many areas in the southern interior and coastal forests.

Identification: Crown symptoms in trees infected by *L. wageneri* are difficult to distinguish from those caused by other root diseases. Reduced leader and branch growth usually occurs quickly accompanied by foliage discoloration and thinning (Fig. 4a). Mortality occurs in "centers" similar to other root diseases. Usually by the time crown symptoms become evident, a purple-brown to black stain can be found in the main lateral roots and the base of the stem. In the stem, the stain occurs as long, tapered streaks (Fig. 4b); in cross-section it appears as narrow bands following the spring wood growth rings (Fig. 4c). Stained sapwood may be resin-soaked.

Microscopic Characteristics: Conidiophores upright, dark coloured, the upper portion with penicilliate branches; conidia hyaline, obovoid, elliptic, or clavate, base usually truncate, 2-8 × 1.7-3.8 µm, held together in a white mucilaginous mass that darkens with age.

Damage: In the interior, up to 50% of the trees have been killed in some lodgepole pine stands 60-110 years of age; infection of Douglas-fir and spruce is less common. On the coast the disease has been reported most frequently in young (15-30 years) stands of Douglas-fir although trees 60 years of age have been killed; infection of western hemlock is rare.

Remarks: Black stain is a vascular wilt; the fungus grows through infected roots in the tracheids preventing water conduction. On reaching the root collar, the fungus grows into uninfected roots and may extend three or more metres up the stem. Local spread occurs through root grafts and infection of feeder roots. Long distance spread has been attributed to root-feeding insects. Black stain root disease may make infected trees attractive to secondary bark beetles such as *Ips* and *Pseudohylesinus* spp. In addition, the fungus may be vectored by root feeding beetles into trees already weakened by *Phellinus weirii* and *Armillaria ostoyae*. In dead trees, the purple-brown to black stain may be obscured by blue stain fungi or sap rots. Blue-stain will appear in a wedge-shaped pattern (Fig. 4d), rather than in bands following annual rings (Fig. 4c). The lower bole and roots of several trees with crown symptoms in an infection center should be examined to determine the cause of the problem. *Atropellis piniphila* also produces a black stain, but is found in stem cankers rather than in roots.

References:
Hunt, R. S. and D. J. Morrison. 1980. Black stain root disease in British Columbia. Can. For. Serv., Forest Pest Leaf. No. 67. Victoria, B.C.
Harrington, T. C. and F. W. Cobb. 1988. Leptographium root diseases on conifers. APS Press, St. Paul, MN.

Figure 4a: Crown thinning of infected lodgepole pine trees. Figure 4b: Black stain visible as longitudinal streaks in Douglas-fir. Figure 4c: Cross-section of black stain, which develops in a pattern that follows the annual rings. Figure 4d: In contrast, blue stain forms radially in a wedge-like pattern.

Schweinitzii Butt Rot

Phaeolus schweinitzii (Fr.:Fr.) Pat.

(= *Polyporus schweinitzii* Fr.:Fr.)

Basidiomycotina, Aphyllophorales, Polyporaceae

Hosts: In B.C., *Phaeolus schweinitzii* has been reported on subalpine and amabilis fir, western larch, tamarack, Sitka and white spruce, lodgepole, **ponderosa** and western white pine, **Douglas-fir**, western redcedar, **western hemlock**, and Garry oak. In other parts of North America it has been found on grand fir, mountain hemlock, black and Englemann spruce, yew, *Acacia* spp., birch, *Eucalyptus*, sweetgum, and *Prunus* spp.

Distribution: This fungus affects trees in all regions of the province.

Identification: Fruiting bodies are annual, generally forming in late summer, and have a spongy, leathery texture They are shelf-like when growing on a stem and stipitate when growing on the ground (Fig. 5a). The upper surface is up to 25 cm in diameter, has concentric rings and is red-brown and velvety, hence the common name "velvet top fungus." The margin of immature sporophores is rounded and is light yellow-green in contrast to the remaining dark area of the upper surface. The lower surface is yellow-green (turning brown when bruised) and poroid; the pores are relatively large and often irregular in outline (Fig. 5b). The context is yellow-green to light brown. Fruiting bodies may persist for a year or more. These turn dark brown in colour but do not continue to produce spores beyond one growing season.

The incipient stage of decay is difficult to recognize and appears as a yellow stain. In the advanced stage of decay, the wood becomes brittle and breaks into large red-brown cubes interspersed with dense white mycelial mats (Figs. 5c, 5d, 5e). The heartwood often disintegrates completely leaving a hollow butt. A characteristic licorice-like odour is often associated with the advanced decay.

Microscopic Characteristics: Contextual hyphae thin-walled, simple septate. Basidiospores ellipsoid to ovoid, hyaline, smooth, IKI-, 6-9 × 2.5-5 µm. Growth in culture rapid, mat yellow-brown, simple-septate, laccase negative. Stalpers: 2 (4) (6) (7) (8) 11 13 14 (17) 19 (21) 25 26 (34) 35 (36) 38 48 (49) 50 52 53 54 55 67 (82) 83 (85) (88) 90 96 97 100.

Damage: Losses to infected trees are relatively high as decay generally occurs in the high quality basal log. In addition, trees with decay are subject to wind-throw or frequently break near their base. In B.C. losses are most severe in Douglas-fir and Sitka spruce.

Remarks: *Phaeolus schweinitzii* causes a butt rot in most mature coniferous tree species, occasionally attacking young trees. Fruiting bodies develop on living and dead trees, on felled timber and on the forest floor near the base of infected trees. Fruiting bodies near the base of trees indicate root infection but not necessarily extensive butt rot. Infected trees should be considered a high risk near buildings and in recreation areas. Advanced decay might be confused with *Fomitopsis pinicola,* or in western redcedar, with *Postia sericeomollis.*

References:

Gilbertson, R. L. and L. Ryvarden. 1987. North American Polypores. 2:539. Fungiflora, Oslo.

Figure 5a: Mature fruiting bodies of *Phaeolus schweinitzii*.
Figure 5b: Pore surface of mature fruiting body.
Figures 5c, 5d, 5e: Advanced decay of Douglas-fir caused by *P. schweinitzii* showing brown cubical rot.

Laminated Root Rot

Phellinus weirii (Murrill) R. L. Gilbertson
(= *Poria weirii* (Murrill) Murrill)
(= *Inonotus weirii* (Murrill) Kotl. & Pouzar)

Basidiomycotina, Aphyllophorales, Polyporaceae

Hosts: Two forms of disease caused by *Phellinus weirii* are recognized, the Douglas-fir and cedar forms, based on cultural characteristics, symptomology, and host preference. It is now generally thought that these "types" represent two different taxa and should have separate names, but more research is required before the nomenclature is finalized. Hosts reported for the Douglas-fir form of *Phellinus weirii* are listed below.

Highly Susceptible	Susceptible	Tolerant	Resistant
Douglas-fir *	California red fir	Lodgepole pine *	Yellow cedar
Grand fir *	Engelmann spruce *	Ponderosa pine *	Incense-cedar
Mountain hemlock	Giant sequoia	Sugar pine	Redwood
Pacific silver fir	Noble fir	Western white pine *	Western redcedar
White fir	Pacific yew		
	Sitka spruce *		
	Subalpine fir *		
	Western hemlock *		
	Western larch *		

* Hosts reported for B.C. Others are from elsewhere in North America.

The cedar form occurs as a butt rot in **western redcedar**, and on Alaska yellow cedar at high elevations at the coast. Deciduous tree species are immune to both forms.

Douglas-fir Form

Distribution: This form is widely distributed throughout the range of Douglas-fir in the province.

Identification: Infected trees may be randomly dispersed throughout a stand or may occur grouped in "disease centers," which are often visible from the air as openings (Fig. 6a). These often appear as patches of young regenerating conifers or resistant hardwood vegetation. The first crown symptoms, a retardation of height and branch growth followed by thinning and yellowing of the foliage are usually not evident until the root system is in an advanced stage of decay. Frequently a stress-induced cone crop will be formed at this stage. The bark of the lower bole sometimes has a darkened, water-stained appearance shortly before or after tree death (Fig. 6b). Basal resinosis is rare. Diseased trees with advanced root decay are frequently windthrown, producing typical "root balls" (Fig. 6c). White to tawny to mauve mycelium (ectotrophic mycelium) can usually be found on or in bark at the root collar and on the roots, particularly in mineral soil. A brown, crust-like mycelial growth often occurs growing over the ectotrophic mycelium on or near the root collar, on infected roots, and on exposed advanced decay (Fig. 6d). This crust like mycelium has the appearance and texture of blistering paint. The rarely produced annual fruiting bodies are brown, crust-like layers on upturned roots and on the underside of decayed logs (Fig. 6e). When fresh, they are light buff with narrow white margins; they turn a uniform dark brown when old and may

Figure 6a: Dead and dying trees in a *Phellinus weirii* disease center. Figure 6b: Bark stain on Douglas-fir.
Figure 6c: Windthrown Douglas-fir in a root-rot center with characteristic root-balls.
Figure 6d: Mauve-coloured ectotrophic mycelium and brown crust-like mycelium on a Douglas-fir root.
Figure 6e: Fruiting body of *P. weirii* on Douglas-fir.

remain in place for 2-3 years. The exposed surface of the fruiting body is poroid; the pores are small and somewhat irregular in outline.

The early stage of decay sometimes appears as a red-brown stain visible on fresh stump tops or cross sections of major roots (Fig. 6f); infection rarely extends more than 1 m up the stem in living trees. Later, stained wood becomes soft and the annual rings separate to form sheets or a typical laminated decay (Fig. 6g); numerous small pits can be seen in the decayed wood. Accumulations of mycelium with reddish-brown setal hyphae (Fig. 6h) usually form between sheets of decayed wood.

Damage: Laminated root rot poses a major threat to its most economically important host, second-growth Douglas-fir. The disease causes root decay, which can cause significant growth reduction, and makes trees susceptible to blowdown and stem breakage (the latter is rare in coastal trees).

Remarks: Initial infection and spread of the fungus in a stand occurs when healthy roots come in contact with diseased roots. The fungus can remain viable in stumps and roots for many decades after tree death thus serving as a source of inoculum for subsequent rotations. Mycelia do not grow freely through the soil and spores are not believed to be important in disseminating the disease. "Disease centers" develop around infected stumps and expand at rates of about 30 cm per year.

Cedar Form

Distribution: *Phellinus weirii* causes a root and butt rot of western redcedar, particularly in old-growth trees throughout the Interior Cedar Hemlock biogeoclimatic zone. It is found to a limited extent on yellow cedar at higher elevations in coastal regions.

Identification: The early stage of decay appears as a yellow-brown stain. Later a laminate, pitted decay is formed (Fig. 6i). Fruiting bodies on cedar are perennial and are typically darker in colour than those of the Douglas-fir form. The pore surface tends to be somewhat smoother and pores are more regular than those found in fruiting bodies of the Douglas-fir form.

Damage: Western redcedar is rarely killed by *P. weirii*, damage being confined mostly to butt rot, which can extend 2-3 m up the bole of living trees; in cases of severe decay, up to 10 m. Most old-growth cedar has some degree of butt rot, much of which is caused by *P. weirii*. This can weaken the tree and lead to stem breakage low on the bole (Fig. 6j).

Microscopic Characteristics: Contextual hyphae thin-walled with frequent branching, simple septate, setal hyphae. Basidiospores hyaline, ovoid, smooth, negative in Melzer's, $4.5-6 \times 3.5-4.5$ µm. Growth in culture moderately rapid, mat white, becoming brown, laccase positive, simple septate, setal hyphae (Fig. 6h) averaging 350 µm (Douglas-fir form), 290 µm (cedar form). Stalpers: 1 3 4 (7) (8) 12 (14) 21 22 30 (31) (33) (34) 35 (37) 48 52 53 54 67 69 83 90. Some culture characteristics differ between the two forms of *P. weirii*. Cedar-type cultures grow slower, and are darker in colour; setal hyphae are shorter and narrower.

References:

Morrison, D. J., M. Merler, and D. Norris. 1992. Detection, recognition, and management of Armillaria and Phellinus root diseases in the southern interior of British Columbia. Can. For. Serv., B.C. Min. For. FRDA Rep. No. 179.

Thies, W. G. and R. N. Sturrock. 1995. Laminated root rot in western North America. USDA For. Serv., CFS Res. Bull. PNW GTR 349.

Wallis, G. W. 1976. *Phellinus (Poria) weirii* root rot detection and management proposals in Douglas-fir stands. Can. For. Serv., For. Tech. Rep. No. 12.

Figure 6f: Incipient decay in outer sapwood of Douglas-fir. Figure 6g: Laminated decay of Douglas-fir typical of *Phellinus. weirii.* Figure 6h: Setal hyphae. Figure 6i: Laminated decay in western redcedar. Figure 6j: Stem breakage on western redcedar caused by *P. weirii* butt rot.

Rhizina Root Rot

Rhizina undulata Fr.:Fr.
(= *Rhizina inflata* (Schaeff.) P. Karst.)

Ascomycotina, Pezizales, Helvellaceae

Hosts: *Rhizina undulata* has been reported in B.C. on western redcedar, Engelmann, Sitka, and white spruce, lodgepole pine, Douglas-fir, western larch, and western hemlock. In other parts of North America, it has also been found on western white pine and grand fir.

Distribution: This disease is prevalent in recently burned sites throughout the province, particularly in the CWH and ICH biogeoclimatic zones.

Identification: Affected seedlings exhibit discoloured foliage or mortality, symptoms similar to other root rots or drought damage (Fig. 7a). Seedlings may be girdled at the root collar. The presence of fruiting bodies (apothecia) within 0.5 m of affected hosts is a good indicator of disease. Apothecia are brown-black, and have a tough, fleshy upper surface that is irregularly lobed and undulating (Fig. 7b). The undersurface is tan-ochre with whitish, cylindrical, branched root-like structures, 1-2 mm thick. The fruiting bodies vary in size, up to 6 cm wide, and may grow together to form a larger mass.

Microscopic Characteristics: Asci about 400×15 µm, J-, ascospores 8/ascus, fusiform with two or more oil drops and a hyaline apiculus at each end, rough, $22\text{-}40 \times 8\text{-}11$ µm.

Damage: Outbreaks of the disease are sporadic, but the mortality of up to 80% of seedlings has been reported in newly established plantations, following site preparation burns. One study reported *Rhizina* damage in one third of 160 stands surveyed in B.C.

Remarks: In B.C., Rhizina root rot is mainly a disease of young seedlings on sites that have been slashburned within 2 years. In other parts of the northern hemisphere, the fungus is known to affect all ages of trees, but is always associated with recent fire activity. Damage might be avoided at high risk sites by delaying planting for two or more years after burning. No chemical or biological controls have been developed. *R. undulata* is sometimes confused with other ascomycete fungi, particularly *Gyromitra* species (Fig. 7c).

References:
Callan, B. E. 1993. Rhizina root rot of conifers. For. Can., Forest Pest Leaf. No. 56. Victoria, B.C.

Ginns, J. H. 1973. Rhizina root rot: severity and distribution in British Columbia. Can. J. For. Res. 4:143-146.

Figure 7a: Seedling mortality and fruiting bodies of *Rhizina undulata*. Figure 7b: *R. undulata* fruiting body. Figure 7c: *Gyromitra* sp. Sometimes confused with *R. undulata*, this fungus does not damage seedlings.

White Butt Rot - White Laminated Rot

Ceriporiopsis rivulosa (Berk. & Curtis) Gilb. & Ryvarden

(= *Poria rivulosa* (Berk. & Curtis) Cooke)
(= *Poria albipellucida* D. Baxter)

Basidiomycotina, Aphyllophorales, Polyporaceae

Hosts: *Ceriporiopsis rivulosa* has been reported in B.C. on **western redcedar**, western hemlock, Douglas-fir, white and Sitka spruce, and amabilis fir. Elsewhere in North America it has also been found on grand fir, sequoia, and in Idaho on larch.

Distribution: This fungus is widely distributed throughout the range of its hosts in B.C.

Identification: The fruiting bodies are annual, thin (up to 3 mm thick), resupinate, poroid and white, forming mostly on slash. They are quite rare and are less useful for identification than are decay symptoms. Fruiting bodies have not been found on sequoia.

The early stage of the decay appears as a yellow discoloration in the heartwood, sometimes surrounded by a blue-to-red stain. Radial cracks may form through the decayed wood as it dries. In the late stage of the decay, the annual rings separate to form coarse laminations or a crumbly mass (Figs. 8a, 8b). Decay symptoms are sometimes not conspicuous in freshly cut logs, but as drying occurs, the wood delaminates along annual rings.

Microscopic Characteristics: Pores angular, 3-4 per mm. Generative hyphae with clamps, irregularly branched. Basidiospores subglobose to oval, hyaline, smooth, IKI-, 5-6 × 6-8 μm.

Growth in culture rapid, mat white, laccase positive, clamp connections, globose-terminal or intercalary chlamysospores. Stalpers: 1 (2) 3 (5) (6) (7) (11) 13 (14) (16) 17 18 21 22 (24) 30 (37) (39) 40 42 45 48 50 52 53 (55) 57 (78) (80) 82 83 (84) 85 (89) (90) (93).

Damage: *Ceriporiopsis rivulosa* is recognized as the most important butt rot of mature western redcedar in the coastal regions of British Columbia. Since decay develops readily early in the life of the tree (when pole-sized), butt logs of mature trees often have significant levels of damage.

Remarks: The decays caused by *C. rivulosa* and the cedar form of *Phellinus weirii* are very similar in gross appearance, particularly in early stages of decay. However, they can be distinguished when laminations form; *C. rivulosa* shows conspicuous, white mycelial flecks between the laminae, and the final stages of decay is crumbly. In contrast, *Phellinus weirii* develops dark brown setal hyphae between the laminations and the wood shows long striations of white cellulose-like material. These striations gives the final decay a fibrous texture. In culture *C. rivulosa* produces clamp-connections whereas *P. weirii* does not.

References:

Buckland, D. C. 1946. Investigations of decay in western Red Cedar in British Columbia. Can. J. For. Res. 24: 158-181.

Gilbertson, R. L. and L. Ryvarden. 1986. North American Polypores. 1:194. Fungiflora, Oslo.

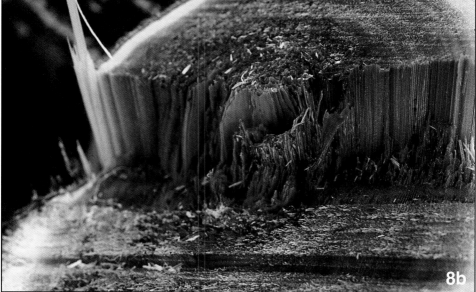

Figure 8a, 8b: Laminate decay in western redcedar caused by *Ceriporiopsis rivulosa.*

Brown Stringy Trunk Rot

Echinodontium tinctorium (Ellis & Everh.) Ellis & Everh.

(= *Fomes tinctorius* Ellis & Everh.)

Basidiomycotina, Aphyllophorales, Hydnaceae

Hosts: In B.C., *Echinodontium tinctorium* has been reported on mountain and **western hemlock, amabilis,** grand and **subalpine fir,** white and Sitka spruce, Douglas-fir, and western redcedar. In other parts of North America it has also been found on larch, Engelmann spruce, and pine True firs are highly susceptible throughout their range, western hemlock is moderately to severely attacked in specific habitats, but Douglas-fir and spruce are seldom attacked. The reports of the fungus on pine and cedar are questionable.

Distribution: Throughout host range in B.C., at high elevations in coastal forests, not reported on the Queen Charlotte Islands; restricted to western North America.

Identification: Sporophores form on living trees, generally in association with branch stubs (Figs. 9a, 9b), and may be up to 30 cm in width. The upper surface of the perennial, hoof-shaped fruiting body is hard, fissured, and generally black. The lower surface bears downward-directed spines, or teeth. These are grey to light-brown when young, turning black with age. The context of the sporophore is brick-red.

The early stage of decay appears as a light brown or water-soaked stain in the heartwood (Fig. 9c). Later the wood darkens to red-brown or yellow-brown. Small rust-coloured flecks and occasionally streaks and white channels, resembling insect tunnels, may develop. Delamination may occur along annual rings (Fig. 9d). Heartwood in advanced decay is reduced to a brown, fibrous, stringy mass which may disintegrate forming a cavity in the tree (Fig. 9e).

Microscopic Characteristics: Hyphae in the context of the fruiting body with clamps, basidiospores smooth-echinulate, hyaline, amyloid, 5.5-8 × 3.5-6 µm. Growth in culture slow, mat white to buff, reverse brown, laccase positive, hyphae with clamps, ellipsoid chlamydospores and clavate cystidia common, Stalpers: 1 2 3 (9) (10) (11) (12) (13) (17) 18 21 (22) (23) 25 30 31 (34) 3(6) 38 39 42 44 (45) 46 48 52 53 (60) 67 (72) 80 (82) 83 85 (88) 90.

Damage: This fungus is the main cause of heart rot and volume loss in mature hemlock and true firs. Sporophores are reliable indicators of defect and are associated with substantial volumes of decay. One fruiting body usually indicates that the entire cross section of the log is decayed for a distance of 2 m above, and 2.5 m below the conk. (Fig. 9f) Decay may also be present in trees that do not bear sporophores.

Remarks: Advanced stages of decay closely resemble equivalent stages of rot associated with *Stereum sanguinolentum*. The common name for *Echinodontium tinctorium*, "Indian paint fungus," is derived from the native Indian use of the ground sporophores in the preparation of red paint pigments. Losses may be reduced by harvesting at pathological rotation age. It has also been suggested that infection might be reduced by inducing natural self-pruning of suppressed branchlets, which are considered to be the major infection courts.

References:

Malloy, O. C. 1991. Review of *Echinodontium tinctorium* Ell. & Ev. [1895-1990]: The indian paint fungus. Wash. St. Univ. Coop. Ext. Serv. EB1592.

Thomas, G. P. 1958. The occurrence of the Indian paint fungus, *Echinodontium tinctorium*, in British Columbia. Studies in For. Path. XVIII. Can. Dept. Ag. Publ. 1041.

Figure 9a: *Echinodontium tinctorium* sporophore associated with a dead branch. Figure 9b: Sporophore with characteristic toothed lower surface. Note the red context colour where the outer surface is chipped away. Figure 9c: Cross-section of early decay symptoms in western hemlock. Figure 9d: Cross-section of advanced decay symptoms. Figure 9e: Longitudinal section of advanced decay showing typical stringy brown rot symptoms. Figure 9f: Cross-section of sporophore associated with a branch and advanced heart rot.

White Spongy Trunk Rot

Fomes fomentarius (L.:Fr.) J. Kickx fil.

Basidiomycotina, Aphyllophorales, Polyporaceae

Hosts: *Fomes fomentarius* has been reported in B.C. on **birch**, alder, balsam poplar, and cotton-wood. Elsewhere in North America it has also been found on maple, Douglas-fir (rarely), oak, apple, willow, and *Prunus* spp.

Distribution: This fungus is widely distributed throughout the range of its hosts in B.C.

Identification: The fruiting bodies are perennial, woody or leathery, and usually hoof shaped (Fig. 10a). The upper surface is zoned (an indicator of perennial growth), grey to brown or grey to black, and smooth with a thick crust. The lower surface is concave, pale-brown, and poroid; the pores are small (4-5 per mm) and regular in outline. The context is a thin brown layer between the surface crust and the old tube layers. Conk age can be fairly accurately estimated as the layers of tubes laid down annually are quite distinct and can be readily counted. Fruiting bodies are found on standing living or dead trees, or on slash.

Decay first appears as a light brown discoloration, the wood remaining quite firm. Wood with advanced decay is yellow-white, soft and spongy, and frequently containing brown to black zone lines (Fig. 10b). Small radial cracks filled with yellow mycelium may develop giving the decay a mottled appearance.

Microscopic Characteristics: Hyphae in the context of the fruiting body thin-walled with clamp connections Basidiospores are cylindric, hyaline, smooth, IKI-, 12-18 (20) × 4-7 µm. Growth in culture rapid, mat first white-cream, then brown, clamp connections, fibre hyphae, laccase positive. Stalpers: 1 2 3 (4) (6) (7) (11) 12 (14) 17 18 21 22 24 25 (26) 30 31 34 (35) (38) 39 42 44 45 36 (47) 48 50 (51) 52 53 (61) (63) 67 83 89 (94).

Damage: *Fomes fomentarius* causes decay in both living and dead timber, producing a white rot that is present in both sapwood and heartwood. If fruiting bodies are visible, there is little merchantable heartwood in a tree.

Remarks: Fungal spread is by air-borne spores, and infection occurs through exposed dead wood tissue. Some control might be achieved by minimizing damage to living trees, and through the removal of dead trees bearing sporophores. The fruiting bodies of *F. fomentarius* might be confused with those of *Phellinus igniarius,* but the upper surface of the former is smoother, lighter in colour, and more "hoof-shaped," with the pore layer generally at an angle of 90° to the tree stem.

References:
Hilborn, M. I. 1942. The biology of *Fomes fomentarius.* Bull. Me. Agric. Exp. Sta. 1942. No. 409.
Stillwell, M. A. 1954. Progress of decay in decadent Yellow Birch trees. For. Chron. 30:292-298.

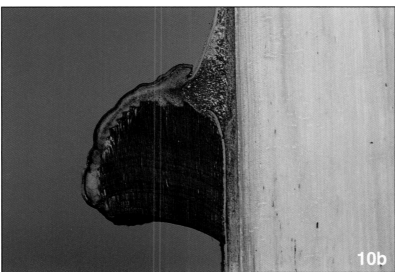

Figure 10a: Fruiting bodies on birch. Figure 10b: A cross-section of a *Fomes fomentarius* fruiting body on a birch stem in an advanced stage of decay.

Brown Trunk Rot

Fomitopsis officinalis (Villars.:Fr.) Bondartsev & Singer

(= *Fomes officinalis* (Villars.:Fr.) Faull.)

(= *Fomes laricis* (Jacq.) Murrill)

Basidiomycotina, Aphyllophorales, Polyporaceae

Hosts: Reported in B.C. on **western larch**, amabilis and grand fir, Engelmann and Sitka spruce, lodgepole, ponderosa, and western white pine, Douglas-fir, and western hemlock. Elsewhere in North America it has also been found on white and black spruce.

Distribution: This fungus is widely distributed throughout the range of its hosts in B.C.

Identification: The fruiting bodies are perennial and vary from hoof-shaped to long pendulous structures (Figs. 11a, 11b). They vary in size from a few to 40 cm in diameter. The upper surface is zoned, white when fresh but drying to dark grey or light brown in old specimens; a chalky coating, which rubs off as a white powder, may be present. The lower surface is white when fresh, drying to light brown, and is poroid; the pores are relatively small and uniform in outline. The context is white or grey, relatively soft when young, toughening with age, and distinctly bitter in taste.

The early stage of decay appears as a light yellow to red-brown stain or, in the case of Douglas-fir, as a purple discoloration. The stain may extend for a considerable distance beyond the advanced decay. In the late stage the wood breaks into brown cubes and thick ($\approx$5 mm) white mycelial felts may form in the shrinkage cracks (Fig. 11c).

Microscopic Characteristics: Hyphae in the context of the fruiting body thin-walled, hyaline, with clamp connections. Basidiospores cylindric-ellipsoid to short-cylindric, hyaline, smooth, IKI-, 6-9 × 3-4 µm. Growth in culture very slow, mat white, laccase negative, chlamydospores common, conidia numerous, borne singly on branches, ovoid, 4.5-7.5 × 3-4.5 µm. Stalpers: (10) (11) (12) 13 14 (15) 17 (18) 21 22 (24) (26) 30 (36) (38) 39 42 45 (51) 52 53 54 (75) (80) 83 85 86 90.

Remarks: Fruiting bodies are formed relatively frequently on larch, and are less common on other species. On all hosts a single fruiting body indicates that most of the wood volume has been destroyed. Trees in recreation areas with conks should be considered high hazard, and should be removed. The decay caused by *F. officinalis* can be confused with other brown cubical rots such as *Laetiporus sulphureus*, *Phaeolus schweinitzii*, or *Fomitopsis pinicola*. *Fomitopsis officinalis*, however, has thicker mycelial mats and is more common higher on the stem. Another distinguishing feature is the bitter taste of the sporophore context and mycelial mats, a characteristic which has given this fungus the common name "quinine fungus."

References:

Gilbertson, R. L. and L. Ryvarden. 1987. North American Polypores. 2:5277. Fungiflora, Oslo.

Figure 11a: Fruiting body of *Fomitopsis officinalis* on western larch. Figure 11b: Eighty-cm assistant with 50-year-old fruiting body. Figure 11c: Advanced decay in western larch.

Brown Crumbly Rot

Fomitopsis pinicola (Sw.:Fr) P. Karst.

(= *Fomes pinicola* (Sw.:Fr.) Cooke)

Basidiomycotina, Aphyllophorales, Polyporaceae

Hosts: *Fomitopsis pinicola* commonly occurs on a wide range of hosts in B.C., including: amabilis, grand, and subalpine fir, Engelmann, white, and Sitka spruce, lodgepole, western white, and ponderosa pine, Douglas-fir, western redcedar, western, mountain, and eastern hemlock, western larch, red alder, paper birch, aspen, cottonwood, plum, and peach. Elsewhere in North America it is also reported on black spruce, cypress, incense and yellow cedar, sequoia, apple, ash, basswood, beech, cherry, chestnut, hickory, magnolia, maple, oak, pear, sycamore, and willow.

Distribution: This fungus is widely distributed throughout the range of its hosts in B.C.

Identification: Fruiting bodies are usually found on dead wood but they occasionally develop on living trees in association with wounds or mistletoe infections. They are perennial, leathery to woody, and hoof-shaped or shelved (Figs. 12a, 12b). The upper surface is usually zoned and has a wide range in colour from dark brown through grey to black. The margin is rounded, often red-brown and lighter than other portions of the upper surface. The lower surface is white to cream and poroid; the pores are circular, 5-6 per mm The context is consistently buff with a tough, corky texture. When fruiting bodies are first developing they appear as firm white masses of fungal material on the bark.

The incipient stage of the decay appears as a yellow-brown to brown stain. Later the wood breaks into small cubes which are soft and crumbly in texture, generally lighter in colour than most crumbly brown rots (12c). Relatively thick white felts of mycelium may form in the shrinkage cracks.

Microscopic Characteristics: Hyphae in the context of the fruiting body of three types: generative hyphae thin-walled with clamps, skeletal, and tramal hyphae thick-walled without septa. Basidiospores cylindric-ellipsoid, hyaline, smooth, IKI-, 6-9 × 3.5-4.5 μm.
Growth in culture slow to moderate, mat white, laccase negative, clamps. Stalpers: (7) (8) (11) (12) (13) 14 (17) (18) 19 21 22 (24) (25) 30 (31) 39 42 (44) 45 46 (47) (48) (51) 52 53 54 (55) 83 85 (88) (89) (90) (93).

Damage: *Fomitopsis pinicola* is one the most damaging decay fungi in old-growth forests. It is a less serious problem in second-growth stands but infected dead trees are subject to wind-throw and top-breakage making them high-risk hazard trees.

Remarks: Brown crumbly rot is one of the most frequently occurring decays in B.C. It occurs frequently as a sap rot but can also gain entrance to the heartwood through wounds and cause considerable damage to living trees. The fungus is very common on dead trees and has a very important ecological role in the degradation of woody forest litter.

References:

Etheridge, D. E. 1973. Wound parasites causing tree decay in British Columbia. Can. For. Serv., Forest Pest Leaf. No. 62. Victoria, B.C.

Figures 12a, 12b: Fruiting bodies of *Fomitopsis pinicola*. Figure 12c: Advanced decay of Douglas-fir by *F. pinicola*. Note brown cubical rot and white mycelium in the cracks of decayed wood.

White Mottled Rot

Ganoderma applanatum (Pers.) Pat.

(= *Fomes applanatus* (Pers.) Gill.)

(= *Polyporus applanatus* (Pers.) Wallr.

Basidiomycotina, Aphyllophorales, Polyporaceae

Hosts: *Ganoderma applanatum* is commonly recorded on deciduous trees, but is also found on a wide range of coniferous tree species. In B.C. it has been reported on maple, alder, birch, beech, apple, poplar, cherry, plum, oak, willow, elm, amabilis and grand fir, white and Sitka spruce, Scots pine, Douglas-fir, mountain and western hemlock, and western redcedar. In other parts of North America, it is found on western white pine, subalpine fir, Engelmann spruce, and many other deciduous hosts (see Farr *et al.*, 1989).

Distribution: This fungus affects trees in all regions of the province.

Identification: The fruiting bodies are perennial, leathery to woody and tend to be flat or plate-like (Fig. 13a). The upper surface is light brown, deeply zoned, and often covered with a dusting of brown spores. The margin, when fresh, is usually white. The context is reddish-brown but may contain a light grey zone. The lower surface is white turning brown in old specimens or when bruised or marked, hence the common names "picture fungus" or "artist's conk."

In the early stage of the decay, the affected wood of most species becomes bleached and is encircled by a dark brown stain. In western hemlock this stage is violet to lilac in colour. In the advanced stage, the wood becomes white, mottled, and spongy (Fig. 13b). Black zone lines may or may not be present.

Microscopic Characteristics: Hyphae in the context of the fruiting body thin-walled with clamp connections, skeletal hyphae thick-walled, brown. Basidiospores ovoid, truncate at the distal end, with two walls, connected by inter-wall pillars, brown, IKI-, (8)9-12 × 8-10 µm. Growth in culture moderately-rapid, mat white, or becoming buff, clamp connections, laccase positive. Stalpers: 1 3 (7) (8) (11) (12) (13) 14 17 18 21 24 25 30 (31) (33) (35) 37 (38) 39 42 44 45 47 (48) (50) 51 52 53 (57) (61) 63 (80) (82) 83 89 (90) (94).

Damage: *Ganoderma applanatum* is an important decay of dead trees but may enter living trees through wounds and cause extensive damage. In hemlock, decay is considered to extend 3 m above and below a sporophore.

Remarks: A related species, *Ganoderma oregonense* (Pers.) Pat, also causes a root and butt rot of living and dead trees in western North America, particularly on true firs and western hemlock. Sporophores of this fungus are often very large (up to 80 cm across), and have a shiny reddish upper surface. Unlike *G. applanatum,* the pore surface does not darken when bruised.

References:

Gilbertson, R. L. and L. Ryvarden. 1986. North American Polypores. 1: 291. Fungiflora, Oslo.

Figure 13a: Fruiting bodies on *Populus* spp. Note the brown spores on the tree bark and upper surface of some of the fruiting bodies. Figure 13b: Advanced decay caused by *Ganoderma applanatum*.

Yellow Pitted Rot

Hericium abietis (Weir ex Hubert) K. A. Harrison
(= *Hydnum abietis* Weir ex Hubert)

Basidiomycotina, Aphyllophorales, Hydnaceae

Hosts: In B.C., *Hericium abietis* causes a butt and trunk rot of **amabilis**, **grand**, and **subalpine fir**, mountain and western hemlock, and occasionally Sitka spruce. Elsewhere in North America it has also been found on Douglas-fir and Engelmann spruce.

Distribution: *Hericium abietis* is restricted to western North America, and is not found east of the Rocky Mountains.

Identification: The fruiting bodies are annual, soft, fleshy, and white, and have many downward-directed spines, 1-2 cm long when fully developed. Spines are produced on a much-branched fleshy stalk (coral-like) (Figs. 14a, 14b).

The early stage of the decay appears as a yellow to brown heartwood stain. Later, elongated pits, about 1 cm long, form, which are oriented longitudinally in the wood (Fig. 14c). These pits are usually empty but may contain yellow to white mycelium. The rot is similar to that of red ring rot (*Phellinus pini*) but with yellow-pitted rot, the pits are usually longer and have blunt ends and the general outline of the decay in cross-section tends to be irregular to honeycomb.

Microscopic Characteristics: Growth in culture relatively slow, mat initially white-tan, then white-yellow-brown, laccase variable and weak, chlamydospores, clamp connections. Basidiospores white, round or nearly so, smooth or minutely roughened, amyloid, 4.5-5.5 × 4-5 μm. Nobles (1965): 2 3 15 34 36 (38) (39) 47 (48) 51 (53) 55 60.

Damage: The presence of a fruiting body indicates extensive decay in the stem. *Hericium abietis* has been reported to reduce merchantable volume by up to 3.1% in amabilis fir.

Remarks: The fruiting bodies are generally found on slash and on the ends of cut logs but they may also form on wounds on living trees. Because of their fleshy nature, they are short lived.

References:
Buckland, D. C., R. E. Foster, and V. J. Nordin. 1949. Studies in forest pathology VII. Decay in western hemlock and fir in the Franklin River area, British Columbia. Can. J. For. Res. 27:312-331.

Filip, G. M., A. M. Kanaskie, and S. J. Frankel. 1984. Substantial decay in Pacific silver fir caused by *Hericium abietis*. Plant Disease 68:992-993.

Ginns, J. H. 1985. *Hericium* in North America: cultural characteristics and mating behavior. Can. J. Bot. 63:1551-1563.

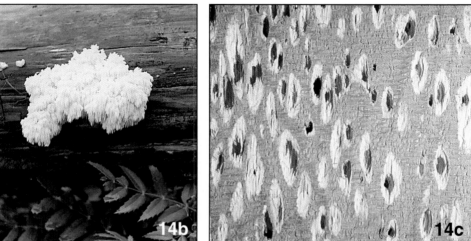

Figures 14a, 14b: Coral-like fruiting bodies of *Hericium abietis*. Figure 14c: Advanced decay:white pocket rot in fir.

Brown Cubical Rot

Laetiporus sulphureus (Bull.:Fr.) Murrill

(= *Polyporus sulphureus* (Bull.:Fr.) Fr.)

Basidiomycotina, Aphyllophorales, Polyporaceae

Hosts: *Laetiporus sulphureus* affects a wide range of coniferous and deciduous hosts. In B.C. it has been reported on **western hemlock**, Engelmann, white and **Sitka spruce**, **Garry oak**, true firs, larch, spruce, ponderosa and western white pine, Douglas-fir, and western redcedar. In other parts of North America it has also been found on lodgepole pine, subalpine and amabilis fir, maple, birch, chestnut, ash, walnut, poplar, *Prunus* spp., pear, willow, sequoia, and elm. In the east it is restricted to deciduous hosts, most commonly oak.

Distribution: This fungus is widely distributed throughout the range of its hosts in B.C.

Identification: The fruiting bodies are annual, spongy to leathery, bracket-like or occasionally stalked, up to 40 cm wide (Figs. 15a, 15b). They often occur in large clusters up to a square metre or more in extent. The upper surface is bright orange-yellow, the context is white to yellow and the lower surface is sulphur yellow with regular pores. Old specimens become brittle when dry and white throughout with a strong, pungent odour. Fruiting bodies seldom form on living coniferous trees but may develop on living deciduous hosts.

The incipient state of the decay appears as a light brown stain. Later the wood breaks into small, red-brown cubes, sometimes having a rippled appearance (Fig. 15c). White, relatively thick mycelial felts may form in the shrinkage cracks within the decay (Fig. 15d).

Microscopic Characteristics: Hyphae in the context of the fruiting body thin-walled, hyaline, simple septate. Basidiospores ovoid to ellipsoid, hyaline, smooth, IKI-, 5-8 × 4-5 µm. Growth in culture moderately rapid, mat white to buff or salmon, laccase negative, clamps always absent. Stalpers: (7) (8) (9) 11 13 14 18 19 (21) 31 (32) (33) 35 48 50 (52) 53 54 55 (80) (82) 83 (84) 85 86 (87) (89) (90).

Damage: Fruiting bodies are often not formed until years after the fungus is well established, so when present, they indicate significant internal defect. The rot is generally restricted to the butt log. When present in recreation sites, infected trees should be considered hazardous and should be removed.

Remarks: The decay caused by *L. sulphureus* is similar to that of *Fomitopsis officinalis*, but the mycelial felts are not bitter. *Laetiporus sulphureus* is a commonly harvested as an edible fungus, easily identified by the morphology and bright yellow colour of its fruiting bodies.

References:

Gilbertson, R. L. and L. Ryvarden. 1986. North American Polypores. 1:424. Fungiflora, Oslo.

Figures 15a, 15b: Fruiting bodies of *Laetiporus sulphureus*.
Figure 15c: Brown cubical rot symptom caused by *L. sulphureus*.
Figure 15d: White mycelial felts associated with decay.

Brown Pocket Rot of Sitka Spruce

Neolentinus kauffmanii (A. H. Smith) Redhead & Ginns

(= *Lentinus kauffmanii* A. H. Sm. in Bier and Nobles.)

Basidiomycotina, Agaricales, Tricholomataceae

Hosts: *Neolentinus kauffmanii* has been reported in B.C. as a butt and trunk decay in **Sitka spruce.** In Washington and Oregon it has also been found on western hemlock.

Distribution: This fungus is restricted to the range of Sitka spruce (i.e., west of the coast mountains).

Identification: The fruiting bodies are small pinkish-tan mushrooms that usually form on exposed advanced decay on fallen or split dead trees (Fig. 16a). Pockets of advanced decay are sharply delimited by apparently sound wood but adjacent pockets may occasionally coalesce to form a continuous column of decay (Fig. 16b). Within the pockets, the wood breaks down into small brown cubes that are soft and friable in texture. (Fig. 16c). In advanced stages, decayed wood crumbles away completely leaving well-defined hollow pockets (Fig. 16d).

Microscopic Characteristics: Hyphae in the context of the fruiting body of two types: generative hyphae 3-10 × 25-160 µm, clamp connections, skeletal hyphae 3-5 × up to 400 µm, gradually tapering. Basidiospores short cylindric, hyaline, thin-walled, IKI-, 4.5-6.7 × 2.5-3.5 µm. Growth in culture moderate to slow, mat white, becoming pinkish-cinnamon buff, laccase negative, clamp connections absent from margin. Nobles: 1 4 8 32 36 44 45 53 55.

Damage: Losses of about 1-2% of gross merchantable volume have been attributed to *Neolentinus kauffmanii* in B.C. It frequently occurs in scattered pockets in the high quality butt log often necessitating the rejection of these logs for lumber production. The amount and pattern of decay visible at the end of a log seldom provides a reliable indication of the extent of internal defect.

Remarks: Decay caused by *N. kauffmanii* cannot be detected in standing timber as the fruiting bodies form only on infected wood exposed to air. The fungus is known to survive in Sitka spruce logs that have been on the ground for more than 50 years.

References:

Bier, J. E. and M. K. Nobles. 1946. Brown pocket rot of Sitka spruce. Can. J. For. Res. 24: 115-120.

Redhead, S. A. and J. H. Ginns. 1985. A reappraisal of agaric genera associated with brown rots of wood. Trans. Mycol. Soc. Japan 26:349-381.

Smith, A. H. 1975. A field guide to western mushrooms. Univ. of Michigan Press. Ann Arbor, MI.

Figure 16a: Fruiting bodies of *Neolentinus kauffmanii*. Figures 16b, 16c, 16d: Characteristic brown pocket-rot symptoms of *N. kauffmanii* in Sitka spruce.

Stringy Butt Rot

Perenniporia subacida (Peck) Donk
(= *Poria subacida* (Peck) Sacc.)

Basidiomycotina, Aphyllophorales, Polyporaceae

Hosts: *Perenniporia subacida* is found in a wide range of coniferous and deciduous hosts. In B.C., it has been reported on **amabilis**, **grand**, and **subalpine fir**, tamarack, **Engelmann, white,** and **Sitka spruce**, lodgepole, Scots, and western white pine, Douglas-fir, **western redcedar, western hemlock,** maple, alder, arbutus, birch, cherry, cottonwood, and willow. Elsewhere in North America it has also been found on mountain hemlock, western larch, juniper, chestnut, tulip-tree, and cypress.

Distribution: This fungus is widely distributed throughout the range of its hosts in B.C.

Identification: The fruiting bodies are perennial, resupinate, and leathery to crust-like (Fig. 17a). The exposed surface is cream to light yellow and poroid; the pores are circular in outline, 5-6 per mm. Fruiting bodies may form on living trees, especially western redcedar, but are generally found on the underside of decayed logs or on the lower stem of dead-standing trees.

The early stage of decay appears as a light brown stain. Later, small white pits develop and coalesce to form a mass of white spongy fibres containing small, black flecks (Fig. 17b). Annual rings may separate to form a laminate decay; yellow-white mycelial mats frequently form between the sheets. The yellow colour of mycelial mats is relatively unique to this fungus. In the final stage, the wood is completely destroyed, leaving a hollow butt (Fig. 17c).

Microscopic Characteristics: Hyphae in the context of the fruiting body thin-walled with clamp connections. Basidiospores ovoid to broadly ellipsoid, hyaline, thin-walled, smooth, IKI-, 4.5-7.5 × 3-5 μm. Growth in culture moderately rapid, mat white, laccase positive, fibre hyphae common. Stalpers: 1 3 (6) (7) (11) (13) (14) 17 19 21 22 24 25 30 37 39 42 44 45 46 (47) 50 51 52 53 54 78 (80) 83 (88) (89) 90.

Damage: The presence of fruiting bodies on living trees indicates up to 3-4 m of defect; on dead trees fruiting bodies indicate almost total cull.

Remarks: Root and butt decay caused by *P. subacida* can cause significant losses and predispose infected trees to wind throw.

References:
Gilbertson, R. L. and L. Ryvarden. 1987. North American Polypores. 2:531. Fungiflora, Oslo.

Figure 17a: *Perenniporia subacida* sporophore on western redcedar.
Figures 17b, 17c: Advanced decay with mycelial mats caused by *P. subacida*.

White Trunk Rot of Conifers

Phellinus hartigii (Allesch. & Schnabl.) Bondartsev

(= *Fomes hartigii* Allesch. & Schnabl.)

(= *Fomes robustus* P. Karst.)

(= *Phellinus robustus* (P. Karst.) Bourd. & Galzin)

Basidiomycotina, Aphyllophorales, Polyporaceae

Hosts: In B.C., *Phellinus hartigii* has been reported on **western hemlock**, amabilis and subalpine fir, and Douglas-fir. In Oregon it has been found on yew.

Distribution: This fungus is widely distributed throughout the range of its hosts in B.C.

Identification: The fruiting bodies are perennial and vary in shape. When formed on the stem, they are hoof-shaped (triangular in longitudinal outline with upper and lower surfaces at angles of 45°), and 5-15 cm wide (Fig. 18a). The upper surface is dark brown to black while the lower surface is brown and poroid. When formed on the lower surface of branches, fruiting bodies are generally resupinate (Fig. 18b). The pores of all fruiting bodies are small (5-7 per mm) and circular in outline.

The decay sometimes occurs as a sector of infected wood extending in from the sapwood. The rot is often found in association with wounds or dead branches and with dwarf mistletoe infections that have killed part of the cambium. Early stages of decay appear as a straw-coloured to purple stain that may be irregular in shape. In the late stages, the wood has a bleached appearance with occasional light brown areas or streaks (Fig. 18c). Zone lines are usually numerous in the decayed wood.

Microscopic Characteristics: Hyphae in the context of the fruiting body thick-walled, aseptate, or rarely simple septate. Setae lacking. Basidiospores globose to subglobose, hyaline, smooth, slightly thick-walled, IKI-, 6-7.5 × 5-6.5 μm. Growth in culture slow, mat white, cream-umber, reverse brown, laccase positive. Stalpers: 1 3 4 (9) (10) (11) (13) 17 21 (22) (25) (30) (34) 35 38 (46) 48 50 52 53 (54) 57 67 80 82 83 90.

Damage: Trees damaged by white trunk rot are prone to wind damage, usually breaking within 6 m of the ground. Decay is usually localized to tissues near the point of infection, but spreads 1-2 m up and down from each fruiting body.

Remarks: The taxonomy of this fungus has been complicated by its morphological variation on different hosts. As a result, many names have been applied to the organism. In the past, many *P. hartigii* specimens were named *Fomes* or *Phellinus robustus*, a name that is now restricted to a related fungus on hardwoods. Another fungus, *Poria tsugina* (Murrill) Sacc. & Trott., now recognized as *Phellinus punctatus* (Fr.) Pilát, has resupinate fruiting bodies that are sometimes confused with those of *P. hartigii*.

References:

Bondartsev, A. S. 1953. The Polyporaceae of the European USSR and the Caucasus. Akad. Nauk SSSR, Moscow.

Gilbertson, R. L. and L. Ryvarden. 1987. North American Polypores. 2:575. Fungiflora, Oslo.

Figures 18a, 18b: Fruiting bodies of *Phellinus hartigii* on a stem (18a), and branch stub (18b) of western hemlock. Figure 18c: Decay caused by *P. hartigii* in a cross-section of a western hemlock branch.

Hardwood Trunk Rot

Phellinus igniarius (L.:Fr.) Quél.
(= *Fomes igniarius* (L.:Fr.) J. Kickx fil.)

Basidiomycotina, Aphyllophorales, Polyporaceae

Hosts: *Phellinus igniarius* is commonly found on many deciduous tree species. In B.C. it has been reported on maple, alder, arbutus, birch, apple, dogwood, cottonwood, locust, and willow. In other parts of North America it has also been found on beech, ash, walnut, cherry, plum, Douglas-fir, pear, oak, and elm.

Distribution: This fungus is widely distributed throughout the range of its hosts in B.C.

Identification: The fruiting bodies are perennial, hard, woody, and generally hoof-shaped, up to 11 cm high × 20 cm wide × 8 cm deep (Figs. 19a, 19b). The upper surface is deeply zoned, grey-black to black and roughened when old. The lower surface is brown and poroid; the pores are small and regular in outline. The context is rust-brown; old tubes are in distinct layers, and are filled with white mycelium that appears as white streaks. Fruiting bodies form on living and dead standing trees and on slash. The presence of a single fruiting body generally indicates a considerable volume of decay.

The early stage of the decay appears as a yellow-white zone in the heartwood, usually surrounded by a yellow-green to brown margin. In the advanced stage the soft yellow-white wood usually contains fine black zone lines running throughout; zone lines also usually surround the decay column (Fig. 19c). Decay symptoms are very similar to those of *Phellinus tremulae*.

Microscopic Characteristics: Pores circular, 5-6 per mm. Hyphae in the context of the fruiting body of two types: thick-walled, aseptate, turning brown in KOH; and thin-walled, hyaline, with occasional simple septa. Hymenial setae abundant to rare, 14-17 × 4-6 µm. Basidiospores broadly ovoid to subglobose, hyaline, smooth, thick-walled, IKI-, 5-6.5 × 4.5-6 µm. Growth in culture moderate, mat white, becoming yellow-brown, laccase positive. Stalpers: 1 3 4 (8) (9) (11) (12) (13) (14) 21 22 (23) (25) (26) 28 (30) (31) (34) 35 (37) (38) (46) 48 (51) 52 53 54 (55) 64 67 (80) 83 89.

Damage: *Phellinus igniarius* is a less aggressive pathogen than other species in the *P. igniarius* complex, but the fungus has an economic impact on host trees grown for timber, pulp, or in recreation sites.

Remarks: A number of similar fungi, including *Phellinus laevigatus*, *P. nigricans*, and *P. tremulae*, were once considered as part of the *Phellinus igniarius* complex, but are now recognized as distinct species. Since the symptoms produced by these fungi are similar, they are often, however, grouped together as the cause of hardwood white trunk rot.

References:
Gilbertson, R. L. and L. Ryvarden. 1987. North American Polypores. 2:576. Fungiflora, Oslo.
Niemlä, T. 1975. On Fennoscandian polypores. IV. *Phellinus igniarius*, *P. nigricans*, and *P. populicola*, n. sp. Ann. Bot. Fennici. 12:93-122.

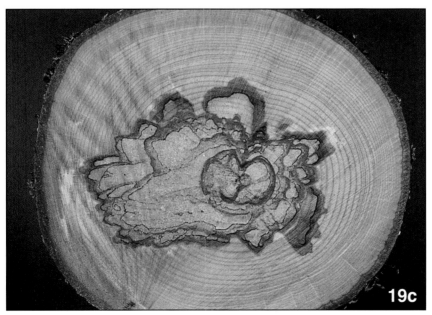

Figures 19a, 19b: *Phellinus igniarius* on willow (19a) and birch (19b). Figure 19c: Decayed wood with zone lines in *P. igniarius*-infected mountain alder.

Red Ring Rot

Phellinus pini (Thore:Fr.) Ames

(= *Fomes pini* (Thore:Fr.) Fr.)

Basidiomycotina, Aphyllophorales, Polyporaceae

Hosts: In B.C., *Phellinus pini* has been reported on amabilis, grand, and subalpine fir, western larch, black, white, Engelmann, and Sitka spruce, jack, lodgepole, ponderosa, and western white pine, Douglas-fir, western redcedar, yellow cedar, and western and mountain hemlock. In other parts of North America it has also been found on maple, alder, birch, yellow cedar, juniper, oak, and yew.

Distribution: This fungus is widely distributed throughout the range of its hosts in B.C.

Identification: Sporophores are hard, woody, perennial, and hoof-shaped to bracket-like or may assume an effused-reflexed form when developing on the lower surface of branches (Figs. 20a-20d). Fruiting bodies range in size up to 9 × 13 × 8 cm. The upper surface is zoned and light to dark brown, with an acute margin. The lower surface is light brown and poroid; the pores are irregular in outline or daedaloid, 2-3 per mm. The context is yellow-brown. Punk knots and swollen knots, which are filled with a yellow-brown mycelial mass represent early or abortive stages in the development of the sporophore.

The incipient stage of decay appears as a red stain in the heartwood (Fig. 20e). In cross section, a well-defined ring often forms, hence the common name "red ring rot." As decay develops, spindle-shaped zones of white fibers are produced running parallel to the grain (Fig. 20f). The surrounding wood is discoloured but firm. The presence of these characteristic white pockets has led to a number of additional common names including honeycomb rot, white pocket rot, or white pitted rot. Dark zone lines may be present.

Microscopic Characteristics: Hyphae in the context of the fruiting body simple septate, hymenial setae abundant, 40-50 × 10-14 µm, basidiospores IKI-, 4.5-7 × 3.5-5 µm. Culture growth slow, mat white to buff, yellow or brown, reverse darker, laccase positive, Stalpers: 1 3 (4) (8) (9) (12) (13) (14) (17) 21 22 (26) 30 (31) 34 35 38 48 52 53 54 67 69 (78) 80 83 90.

Damage: Sporophores are produced on living trees and may provide a general guide to the amount and distribution of internal decay within one tree species and region. Sporophores often develop adjacent to branch stubs and, in cases of extensive infection, may form more or less along the length of the bole. Decay can progress from the heartwood to the sapwood and cause tree death. Tests of wood strength suggest no significant weakening during incipient decay, and rot is not known to develop in wood in service.

Remarks: The fruiting bodies of *P. pini* vary considerably in morphology, on different hosts. *Phellinus pini* might be confused with early incipient decay caused by *Echinodontium tinctorium*, or the natural reddish discoloration in some pines. Other fungi also produce a white pocket rot; *Phellinus nigrolimitatus* and *Hericium abietis* produce larger pockets with well-defined margins, *Inonotus tomentosus* and *Dichomitus squalens* (P. Karst) D. Reid form pockets with poorly defined margins.

References:

Blanchette, R. A. 1980. Decay and canker formation by *Phellinus pini* in white and balsam fir *Abies concolor, Abies balsamea*. Can J. For. Res. 12:538-544.

Figures 20a-20d: *Phellinus pini* fruiting bodies on pine (20a), western hemlock (20b), and Douglas-fir (20c, 20d). Figure 20e: Incipient red stain in the heartwood of pine. Figure 20f: White pocket rot characteristic of *P. pini.*

Aspen Trunk Rot

Phellinus tremulae (Bondartzev) Bondartzev & Borisov in Bondartzev

(= *Fomes igniarius* (L.:Fr.) J. Kickx fil. f. *tremulae* Bondartzev)

(= *Fomes igniarius* var. *populinus* (Neuman) Camp.)

Basidiomycotina, Aphyllophorales, Polyporaceae

Hosts: *Phellinus tremulae* is found only on trembling aspen.

Distribution: This fungus is widely distributed throughout the range of its host in B.C.

Identification: The fruiting bodies are perennial, hard, woody, up to 20 cm wide and 15 cm thick, and generally triangular shaped in longitudinal section (Fig. 21a). The fruiting bodies differ in shape from those of *P. igniarius*; the upper and lower surfaces of *P. tremulae* are at angles of about 45° from horizontal, whereas *P. igniarius* conks are hoof-shaped with the lower surface close to horizontal. The upper surface is deeply zoned, grey-black to black and roughened when old. The lower surface is brown and poroid; the pores are small and regular in outline. The context is rust-brown; old tubes are in distinct layers, and are filled with white mycelium that appears as white streaks. Fruiting bodies form in association with branch scars on living and dead standing trees and on slash. Black, sterile mycelial masses commonly called sterile conks, blind conks, or punk knots also form at branch scars (Fig. 21b).

The early stage of the decay appears as a yellow-white zone in the heartwood, usually surrounded by a yellow-green to brown margin. In the advanced stage the soft yellow-white wood usually contains fine black zone lines running throughout; zone lines also usually surround the decay column (Fig. 21c).

Microscopic Characteristics: Hyphae in the context of the fruiting body of two types: thick-walled, simple septate, dark reddish-brown, and thin-walled, pale-yellow to hyaline, with simple septa. Hymenial setae present, 12-30 × 6-7.5 μm. Basidiospores subglobose, hyaline, smooth, IKI-, 4.5-5 × 4-4.5 μm. Growth in culture slow, mat white, becoming buff, then brown, laccase positive, strong odour of wintergreen. Stalpers: 1 3 4 (9) (10) (11) (12) (13) (14) (15) (17) 21 22 (25) (26) 28 (30) (31) (34) 35 36 (38) (46) 48 51 52 53 64 67 (80) 83 89.

Damage: Aspen trunk rot is one of the most serious problems limiting the utilization of mature aspen in western Canada. The presence of a single fruiting body generally indicates a considerable volume of decay, as much as 82% of gross tree volume. Unfortunately, there are often no external indicators of decay, and it is difficult to predict decay volumes. Volume losses increase significantly with tree age.

Remarks: *Phellinus tremulae* was once considered as a part of the *Phellinus igniarius* complex, but is now recognized as distinct species. It occurs exclusively on aspen, and is the most damaging decay fungus associated with the tree species. Decayed wood in fresh cut trees has a distinct wintergreen odour.

References:

DeByle, N. V. and R. P. Winokur (eds). 1985. Aspen: ecology and management in the western United States. USDA For. Serv., Gen. Tech. Rep. RM-119.

Gilbertson, R. L. and L. Ryvarden. 1987. North American Polypores. 2:614. Fungiflora, Oslo.

Hinds, T. E. and E. M. Wengert. 1977. Growth and decay losses in Colorado aspen. USDA For. Serv., Res. Paper RM-193.

Hiratsuka, Y. and A. A. Loman. 1984. Decay of aspen and balsam poplar in Alberta. Can. For. Serv., Inf. Rep. No. NOR-X-262.

Figure 21a, Fruiting body of *Phellinus tremulae.* Figure 21b: Aspen trees with "blind conks."
Figure 21c: Cross- and longitudinal-section of decayed aspen stem infected with *P. tremulae* (note conk).

Yellow Laminated Butt Rot of Poplars

Pholiota populnea (Pers.:Fr.) Kuyper & Tjall.-Beukers
(= *Pholiota destruens* (Brond.)

Basidiomycotina, Agaricales, Strophariaceae

Hosts: *Pholiota populnea* has been reported in B.C. on black cottonwood and Lombardy poplar.

Distribution: This fungus is widely distributed throughout the range of its hosts in B.C.

Identification: The fruiting bodies are relatively large, gilled mushrooms, often occurring in clusters, which develop on living trees or slash. When fresh, the cap is light brown and covered with white scales (Fig. 22a). The gills are white when immature, becoming dark brown as spores mature. The stem is white to light brown and covered with white scales; a white annulus is present. The mushrooms are abundant from midsummer to late autumn.

In the early stage the decay appears as buff to dark brown streaks in the heartwood. Later white patches form giving the wood a faint mottled appearance. In the final stage, the wood becomes uniformly yellow to tan and laminate in texture.

Microscopic Characteristics: Basidiospores cinnamon-brown, elliptical, smooth, with a germ pore, 7-9.5 × 4-5.5 µm. Chrysocystidia absent.

Damage: Although no detailed decay-volume loss studies have been conducted, *P. populnea* is thought to cause more loss than any other decay fungus on cottonwood.

Remarks: The fungus seems to be most damaging in living trees, only remaining active in stumps and logs for a few years following harvest.

References:

Thomas, G. P. and D. G. Podmore. 1953. Decay in Black Cottonwood in the middle Fraser region, British Columbia. Can. J. Bot. 31: 675-692.

Figure 22a: *Pholiota populnea* fruiting body on a cut log.

Brown Cubical Rot of Birch

Piptoporus betulinus (Bull.:Fr.) P. Karst.

(= *Polyporus betulinus* (Bull.:Fr.) Fr.)

Basidiomycotina, Aphyllophorales, Polyporaceae

Hosts: *Piptoporus betulinus* is restricted to birch; white birch in B.C. and yellow birch elsewhere.

Distribution: This fungus is found throughout the range of birch in the province.

Identification: The fruiting bodies are annual, leathery, with a short, stout stipe, and a cap up to 15 cm deep, × 25 cm wide × 6 cm high (Fig. 23a). The upper surface is light brown, becoming darker brown and scaly, with a margin that extends below the pore surface. The pore surface is white, becoming light brown and slightly tooth-like with age (Fig. 23b), pores circular, 3-5 per mm. Context white, easily separating from tube layer when fresh.

Decayed wood is yellowish-brown and cracks into cubes with thin white mycelial mats forming in the cracks. Wood in advanced stages of decay is very light in weight and easily crumbles to powder.

Microscopic Characteristics: Hyphae in the context of the fruiting body of two types: thin-walled, hyaline with clamp connections, and thick-walled, aseptate Basidiospores cylindric, allantoid, hyaline, smooth, IKI-, 5-6 × 1.5-1.7 μm. Growth in culture moderately rapid, mat colourless to white, forming compact balls of mycelium on surface of medium, chlamydospore-like swellings, laccase negative. Stalpers: (6) (7) (12) (13) 14 17 19 21 (22) 30 (31) 80 83 (85) (88) 89 (93).

Damage: *Piptoporus betulinus* is often present in dead branches of dying trees. After trees die, rot develops in the bark and sapwood, and generally spreads to the centre of the trunk. Infected wood decays rapidly; laboratory studies have shown reduction of wood density of 30-70% in four months.

Remarks: *Piptoporus betulinus* is one of the few brown rotting fungi that only attacks hardwoods. Although it is restricted to birch hosts in nature, other tree species such as pine, spruce, and poplar have been successfully inoculated in lab and field experiments.

References:
Gilbertson, R. L. and L. Ryvarden. 1987. North American Polypores. 2:633. Fungiflora, Oslo.

Figure 23a: *Piptoporus betulinus* fruiting body on a dead standing birch stem.
Figure 23b: Older fruiting bodies on a fallen birch stem.

Brown Cubical Butt and Pocket Rot of Cedar

Postia sericeomollis (Romell) Jülich

(= *Oligoporus sericeomollis* (Romell) Pouz.)
(= *Polyporus sericeomollis* Romell)
(= *Poria sericeomollis* (Romell) Egeland)
(= *Poria asiatica* (Pilát) Overh.)

Basidiomycotina, Aphyllophorales, Polyporaceae

Hosts: In B.C., *Postia sericeomollis* has been reported on most conifers including **western red-cedar**, subalpine fir, western larch, Engelmann, white, and Sitka spruce, lodgepole and ponderosa pine, Douglas-fir, yellow cedar, and western hemlock. Elsewhere in North America it has also been found on grand fir, western white pine, juniper, and cherry.

Distribution: This fungus is widely distributed throughout the range of its hosts in B.C.

Identification: The fruiting bodies are annual, resupinate, thin, up to 15 cm wide, and white. They rarely, if ever, appear on living trees but form on the ends of logs or on slash (Fig. 24a).

The incipient decay is straw-coloured to pale yellow-brown. Later the wood turns light brown, becomes brittle, and breaks down into cubes to form a cylinder of rot (usual when in the butt) or a series of isolated pockets that may run together to form arcs or concentric rings of decayed wood (Figs. 24b-24e). A thin, white weft of mycelium may sometimes form between the cubes.

Microscopic Characteristics: Hyphae in the fruiting body hyaline, thin or thick-walled, with abundant clamp connections. Basidiospores oblong to cylindric-ellipsoid, hyaline, smooth, IKI-, 4-5 × 2-2.5 µm. Growth in culture very slow, mat white, chlamydospores with thick rough walls, laccase negative. Stalpers: (8) (9) (10) 11 (12) (13) 14 17 (19) 21 22 (23) (25) 30 (31) 36 39 42 44 45 (48) 52 53 54 83 85 90.

Damage: This decay is very common in the butt logs of western redcedar, resulting in significant volume losses in both interior and coastal trees. Brown cubical rot symptoms are commonly found in cedar lumber (Fig. 24e) but the decay is not known to develop further in wood in service.

Remarks: Cedar pocket rot is an important butt and trunk decay of western redcedar, ranking second to *Phellinus weirii* as the most common decay in that species. *Postia sericeomollis* could be confused with *Phaeolus schweinitzii*. Decay in the former, however, usually forms in pockets or rings of decay, whereas *P. schweinitzii* usually forms a single column of decay in the centre of the stem. This distinction may be less clear in the stump than higher in the stem. In addition, *P. schweinitzii* is rarely found in western redcedar.

References:

Buckland, D. C. 1946. Investigations of decay in western redcedar in British Columbia. Can. J. Bot. 24:158-181.

Figure 24a: Resupinate sporophore of *Postia sericeomollis* on western redcedar.
Figures 24b, 24c, 24d: Brown cubical rot in western redcedar. Figure 24e: Brown cubical rot in cedar lumber.

Brown Stringy Trunk Rot of Hardwoods

Spongipellis delectans (Peck) Murrill

(= *Polyporus delectans* Peck)

Basidiomycotina, Aphyllophorales, Polyporaceae

Hosts: *Spongipellis delectans* is an important decay of **black cottonwood**, and has only been found on this species in B.C. In other parts of North America it has been reported on maple, alder, and oak.

Distribution: This fungus is most likely found wherever cottonwood is present but has been poorly collected to date.

Identification: The fruiting bodies are annual, fleshy to leathery, up to 7 cm deep × 15 cm wide × 4.5 cm high, and of various shapes, but usually shelved (Fig. 25a). The upper and lower surfaces and the context are white when fresh, drying to light brown. The lower surface is poroid, the pores are small and regular in outline.

The decay first becomes apparent as buff to light brown streaks in the heartwood. In the advanced stage of the decay, the wood becomes light in weight, uniformly dark brown, usually stringy but sometimes laminate (Fig 25b). Initially the decay will form pockets of various sizes but in time these usually come together to form a column (Fig. 25c).

Microscopic Characteristics: Hyphae in the context of the fruiting body hyaline, thin and thick-walled, with clamp connections. Basidiospores broadly ellipsoid to subglobose, hyaline, smooth, IKI-, 7-9 × 5-7 µm. Growth in culture moderate, mat white, laccase positive. Stalpers: 1 3 (6) (7) (8) (11) (12) (13) (14) 21 22 30 (39) 40 42 (44) (45) (50) 52 (54) (58) (60) (61) (78) 80 (82) 83 84 85 (88) 89 (94) (95) (96) 97 100.

Damage: Significant losses in wood strength occur in trees with advanced decay.

Remarks: Decay occurs mainly as a trunk rot, rarely as a butt rot, in both living and dead trees. In living trees, decay is usually confined to the heartwood. Infection appears to occur through branch stubs or branch scars.

References:

Gilbertson, R. L. and L. Ryvarden. 1987. North American Polypores. 2:723. Fungiflora, Oslo.

Thomas, G. P. and D. G. Podmore. 1953. Decay in Black Cottonwood in the middle Fraser region, British Columbia. Can. J. Bot. 31: 675-692.

Figure 25a: Fruiting bodies of *Spongipellis delectans* on a cottonwood stump.
Figures 25b, 25c: Advanced decay symptoms caused by *S. delectans*.

Red Heart Rot

Stereum sanguinolentum (Albertini & Schwein.:Fr.) Fr.

(= *Haematostereum sanguinolentum* (Albertini & Schwein.:Fr.) Pouzar))
(= *Stereum balsameum* Peck)

Basidiomycotina, Aphyllophorales, Stereaceae

Hosts: In B.C., *Stereum sanguinolentum* has been reported on lodgepole, ponderosa, and western white pine, white and Engelmann spruce, western redcedar, western and mountain hemlock, Douglas-fir, western larch, tamarack, and subalpine, amabilis, and grand fir. In other parts of North America it has also been found on Sitka spruce, alder, and *Amelanchier*.

Distribution: This fungus is widely distributed throughout the range of its hosts in B.C.

Identification: Fruiting bodies (Figs. 26a, 26b) are common on the lower side of fallen dead branches, log ends and on the face of infected wounds and are occasionally found on dead standing trees. They are annual, leathery, and resupinate to effused-reflexed, often forming thin, crust-like layers. In the effused-reflexed form, the upper surface is grey to light brown and zoned the lower surface is wrinkled, grey to light brown, turning blood red when bruised, hence the common name "bleeding fungus."

The incipient stage of the decay is firm and appears as a red-brown heartwood stain. In the advanced stage the wood becomes light brown to red-brown and soft and fragile in texture. Thin white mycelial fragments may develop in association with advanced decay. Finally, the wood becomes a brown, fibrous, stringy mass.

Microscopic Characteristics: Hyphae in the context of the fruiting body thin-walled, hyaline to pale-yellow, simple septate, or thick-walled, rarely septate. Basidiospores are hyaline, cylindrical, smooth, amyloid. Basidiospore size varies among specimens, either large (8-14 × 3-5 µm,) or more commonly, small. (5-7 × 2-3.5 µm). Growth in culture moderate, mat white to buff, laccase positive, multiple clamp connections present. Stalpers: (1) 3 (7) (8) (11) (12) (13) 14 (15) 17 (18) (19) 21 (22) 24 (25) 30 31 (34) (35) (36) (38) (39) (40) 41 42 44 (48) 50 (51) 52 53 54 (60) (67) (73) (82) 83 90 (92) 96 98 100.

Damage: Red heart rot is responsible for extensive heart rot in mature pine, spruce, and true firs. In other hosts it is largely a slash-destroyer, although it may occasionally be responsible for heartwood stain and terminal die-back.

Remarks: *Stereum sanguinolentum* is commonly associated with pruning wounds, logging scars, and lesions formed as a result of climatic injury. It has also been reported to gain entry through root injuries. Fruiting bodies of *S. sanguinolentum* can be distinguished from those of *Chondrostereum purpureum*, a fungus that appears somewhat similar, by the deep red colour of the bruised lower surface of the former. In addition, *S. sanguinolentum* is usually found on conifers, *C. purpureum* on hardwoods.

References:

Etheridge, D. E. 1973. Wound parasites causing tree decay in British Columbia. Can. For. Serv., Forest Pest Leaf. No. 62. Victoria, B.C.

Nakasone, K. K. 1990. Cultural studies and identification of wood-inhabiting Corticiaceae and selected Hymenomycetes from North America. J. Cramer, Berlin.

Lentz, P. L. 1955. *Stereum* and allies genera of fungi in the upper Mississippi valley. USDA For. Serv., Agric. Mon. 24.

Figures 26a, 26b: Fruiting bodies of *Stereum sanguinolentum*.

Brown Cubical Pocket Rot

Veluticeps fimbriata (Ellis & Everh.) Nakas.

(= *Hymenochaete fimbriata* Ellis & Everh.)
(= *Stereum rugisporum* (Ellis & Everh.) Burt)

Basidiomycotina, Aphyllophorales, Corticiaceae

Hosts: In B.C., *Veluticeps fimbriata* has been reported mainly on western hemlock, amabilis, grand, and subalpine fir, but also on mountain hemlock, Douglas-fir, and Engelmann and Sitka spruce. In other parts of North America it has also been found on western redcedar, white and black spruce, western larch, and pine.

Distribution: This fungus is widely distributed throughout the range of its hosts in B.C.

Identification: The perennial fruiting bodies are small and resupinate or shelf-like with a roughened grey to light brown lower surface and a dark brown to nearly black upper surface. The context is brown. The hymenial surface is smooth to warted, and usually cracked to some extent. Fruiting bodies may form on the scarred faces of living trees but more frequently are found on old logs and dead material on the ground (Fig. 27a).

The early stage of decay is characterized by a wet, dark brown or black stain that occurs in streaks or patches. The advanced stage develops in pockets surrounded by what appears to be sound wood. In the final stage the individual pockets coalesce, forming an almost continuous column of decay (Fig. 27b). The decay is soft and friable and is often associated with dark stain, a thin cobweb-like accumulation of mycelium and an odour resembling that of stored apples.

Microscopic Characteristics: Contextual hyphae in five distinct layers, clamp connections present. Basidiospores ellipsoid to cylindrical, hyaline, but occasionally pale yellow, slightly thick-walled, smooth, IKI-, 11.9-15.5 × 4.7-5.6(-6) μm. Growth in culture very slow, mat becoming brown, reverse brown, conspicuous opaque brown dots in agar, laccase negative, simple septa, globose to oblong chlamydospores. Stalpers: (1) 2 (9) (10) (11) 13 (14) (16) 17 (21) 22 (30) (31) 34 38 (39) (40) 42 45 48 (49) (50) 52 53 (54) (60) 61 67 (72) 75 80 83 85 90 96 98.

Damage: *Veluticeps fimbriata* was once considered to be only a slash destroyer, but is now recognized as a commonly occurring trunk rot in conifers. The fungus is also capable of continued development in unseasoned timber.

Remarks: Collections of this fungus were previously identified as *Columnocystis abietina* (= Stereum *abietinum* Pers.), but a recent taxonomic study by Nakasone (1990) has split the group, and treats the collections from B.C. as *V. fimbriata*.

References:

Nakasone, K. K. 1990. Taxonomic study of *Veluticeps* (Aphyllophorales). Mycologia 82: 622-641.

Figure 27a: Fruiting bodies of *Veluticeps fimbriata* on a fallen western hemlock log.
Figure 27b: Advanced decay of western hemlock caused by *V. fimbriata*.

Spruce Broom Rust

Chrysomyxa arctostaphyli Dietel

Basidiomycotina, Uredinales, Coleosporiaceae

Hosts: In B.C. the aecial hosts of *Chrysomyxa arctostaphyli* are white, black, Norway, Engelmann, and Sitka spruce. Elsewhere it is reported on blue and red spruce. The telial host is kinnikinnick.

Distribution: This fungus is widely distributed throughout the range of its hosts in B.C.

Identification: Spruce infected with *C. arctostaphyli* form conspicuous, perennial brooms (Figs. 28a, 28b, 28c). These may be up to 2 m in diameter and form anywhere in the crown of the tree. During the spring, brooms start out pale green, a result of needle chlorosis, then appear orange in mid-summer when the aecia are formed (Fig. 28d). Needles in the broom are shed in the fall. Telia form on the lower surfaces of kinnikinnick leaves, appearing as crowded groups of localized reddish-brown spots (Fig. 28e, 28f).

Microscopic Characteristics: Spermogonia and aecia on current years needles. Aeciospores 16-25 × 23-35 µm, wall 2-3 µm thick with columnar warts. Uredinia lacking. Telia hypophyllous, reddish-brown. Teliospores 13-18 × 23-64 µm.

Damage: Spruce brooms are often associated with stem deformations, reduced increment growth, broken tops, and tree mortality. Rust brooms also serve as infection courts for decay fungi such as *Phellinus pini*, contributing to increased levels of damage.

Remarks: The brooming symptoms caused by *C. artcostaphyli* could be confused with mistletoe infections. However, distinguishing features of the rust are the complete loss of needles in the winter and the yellow-orange colour of the broom in the spring and summer.

References:

Baranyay, J. A. and W. G. Ziller. 1972. Broom rusts of conifers in British Columbia. Can. For. Serv., Forest Pest Leaf. No. 48. Victoria, B.C.

Peterson, R. S. 1963. Effects of broom rusts on spruce and fir. USDA For. Serv., Res. Paper INT-7.

Ziller, W. G. 1974. The tree rusts of western Canada. Can. For. Serv., Publ. No. 1329. Victoria, B.C.

Figure 28a: Spruce broom associated with a dead top caused by *Chrysomyxa arctostaphyli*. The broom appears dead, with no needles, during the winter months. Figures 28b, 28c: Spruce broom with sporulating aecia on needles. Figure 28d: Sporulating aecia. Figure 28e: Kinnikinnick, the telial host of *C. arctostaphyli*. Discoloured spots on the upper surface of the leaves indicate the presence of telia on the lower surface. Figure 28f: Telia on the lower surface of kinnikinnick leaves.

Large-Spored Spruce-Labrador Tea Rust

Chrysomyxa ledicola Lagerh.

Basidiomycotina, Uredinales, Coleosporiaceae

Hosts: The aecial hosts of *Chrysomyxa ledicola* in B.C. include white, black, Sitka, and Englemann spruce. The telial hosts are Labrador-tea and northern Labrador-tea.

Distribution: This disease is common throughout the province and affects spruce in areas where the alternate host is present. Its occurrence on *Ledum*, however, is not restricted to areas where spruce occurs.

Identification: *Chrysomyxa ledicola* is the most common of the non-brooming needle rusts of spruce. Blister-like aecia form on current years needles, and occasionally on cone scales, producing orange-coloured aeciospores throughout the summer (Figs. 29a, 29b). *C. ledicola* is easily recognized on the alternate host, Labrador-tea, since it is the only rust that produces uredinia on the upper surface of the leaves (Fig. 29c).

Microscopic Characteristics: Spermogonia amphigenous, aecia hypophyllous; on current years needles, rarely on cone scales. Aecia orange with fragile white peridium. Aeciospores broadly ellipsoid, 22-34 × 27-46, walls colourless, 3-6 µm thick, coarsely verrucose, warts stellate in surface view. Uredinia and telia epiphyllous on previous years foliage. Uredinia orange. Urediniospores broadly ellipsoid or globoid, 20-33 × 24-45 µm, wall colourless, 1.4-4.8 µm thick, warts nearly cylindrical to fluted. Telia epiphyllous, flat, 10-24 × 13-18 µm, wall colourless, uniformly 1 µm thick.

Damage: Severe defoliation of spruce occurs in localized areas, particularly when moist environmental conditions prevail.

Remarks: A similar rust on spruce, small-spored spruce-Labrador-tea rust, caused by *Chrysomyxa ledi* de Bary var. *ledi*, differs from *C. ledicola* in that its aeciospores are smaller (13.5-25 x 18-32 µm) and that uredinia form on the lower surface of *Ledum* leaves.

References:
Savile, D. B. O. 1950. North American species of *Chrysomyxa*. Can J. For. Res. 28:318-330.
Ziller, W. G. 1974. The tree rusts of western Canada. Can. For. Serv., Publ. No. 1329. Victoria, B.C.

Figures 29a, 29b: *Chrysomyxa ledicola* aecia on spruce needles. Figure 29c: *C. ledicola* uredinia on the upper surface of Labrador-tea leaves.

Spruce Cone Rusts

Inland spruce cone rust
Chrysomyxa pirolata G. Wint. in Rabenh.

Coastal spruce cone rust
Chrysomyxa monesis Ziller

Basidiomycotina, Uredinales, Coleosporiaceae

Hosts: In B.C., the aecial hosts of *Chrysomyxa pirolata* are limited to spruce species, including Engelmann, white, black, Colorado, and Sitka spruce. Elsewhere in North America it has been reported on red spruce. The telial hosts include single delight and a number of species of wintergreen where the rust is systemic and perennial.

Chrysomyxa monesis is restricted to Sitka spruce as an aecial host and single delight as a telial host.

Distribution: *Chrysomyxa pirolata* is found throughout the province, whereas *C. monesis* occurs only at the coast on spruce and both at the coast and in the interior on single delight.

Identification: *Chrysomyxa pirolata* and *C. monesis* attack only the cones of spruce, not the needles. Infected cones turn brown prematurely and are easily identified by the presence of orange-coloured aeciospores, which form between the cone scales in late summer (Figs. 30a, 30b, 30c). A light "dusting" of aeciospores is often observed on vegetation beneath trees with diseased cones. Yellow uredinia are present on the lower leaf surfaces, and sometimes on the petioles of the telial hosts (Figs. 30d, 30e). *Chrysomyxa pirolata*-infected leaves of *Pyrola* spp. are slightly chlorotic, more erect, and the upper surface is less shiny than that of healthy leaves. *Chrysomyxa monesis*-infected *Moneses uniflora* plants may be slightly chlorotic, but commonly show no symptoms.

Microscopic Characteristics: *Chrysomyxa pirolata:* Spermogonia and aecia on cone scales, aecia yellow-orange. Aeciospores broadly ellipsoid, clear, thick walls, warts depressed, forming a reticulate pattern, 17-35 × 22-37 µm (Fig. 30f). Uredinia hypophyllous, systemic, round, yellowish-red. Urediniospores with yellow contents, ellipsoid, clear walls with warts resembling those of aeciospores, 13-24 × 19-33 µm. Telia hypophyllous, flat, orange-brown.

Chrysomyxa monesis: Spermogonia and aecia on cone scales, aecia yellow-orange. Aeciospores broadly ellipsoid, clear, thick walls, warts narrow, deeply fluted, 17-25 × 29-45 µm. Uredinia hypophyllous, systemic, round, yellowish-red. Urediniospores with yellow contents, ellipsoid, clear walls with warts resembling those of aeciospores, 15-22 × 23-34 µm. Telia hypophyllous and on petioles, waxy, yellow turning brown with age.

Damage: These rusts periodically damage cones in localized forest areas and can be a serious problem in spruce seed orchards.

Remarks: Seeds are not usually formed in diseased cones, and even when they are produced, malformation and resinosis of the cones hinder seed dispersal or extraction. Those seeds that are formed tend to weigh less and have poor germination.

References:
Sutherland, J. R., T. Miller, and R. S. Quinard. 1987. Cone and seed diseases of North American conifers. N. Am. For. Commis., Publ. No.1.

Ziller, W. G. 1974. The tree rusts of western Canada. Can. For. Serv., Publ. No. 1329. Victoria, B.C.

Figures 30a, 30b, 30c: *Chrysomyxa pirolata* aeciospores produced beneath the cone scales of spruce cones. Figure 30d: *C. pirolata* uredinia on the lower surface of a wintergreen leaf. Figure 30e: Orange-yellow urediniospores produced in uredinial pustules. Figure 30f: *C. pirolata* urediniospores.

Stalactiform Blister Rust

Cronartium coleosporioides Arthur

(= *Cronartium stalactiforme* Arth. & Kern)

Basidiomycotina, Uredinales, Cronartiaceae

Hosts: *Cronartium coleosporioides* is restricted to pine, specifically the two- and three-needle, hard pines. In B.C., it is found on lodgepole, ponderosa, and jack pine in natural forests, and on any of the introduced hard pines including bishop, mugo, Monterey, Scots, and Austrian pines. The main alternate hosts are paintbrush (Fig. 31a), and cow-wheat (Fig. 31b). Other alternate hosts that have been identified by artificial inoculation are: yellow owl's clover, bracted louse-wort, and yellow-rattle.

Distribution: This fungus is found throughout the range of its hosts in B.C., but is limited to areas where both aecial and telial hosts occur.

Identification: Perennial cankers, which form on stems and branches of the pine host, are generally elongate (up to and over 10 times longer than broad), diamond-shaped, and often girdle smaller stems and branches (Figs. 31c, 31d). Bark tissue may be thickened resulting in fusiform swelling. During late spring and summer, aecia appear as white-orange blisters that release orange aeciospores. During other times of the year, *C. coleosporioides* infections may be identified by their size, shape, and by sunken, dead bark and resinosis associated with the cankers. Porcupines and other rodents often preferentially chew on cankers during the winter leaving exposed wood (Fig. 31e).

Microscopic Characteristics: Spermatia and aecia on pine caulicolous, spermatia ovoid. Aecial filaments on inner surface of peridium pendant (Fig. 31f). Aeciospores orange, ellipsoid, 17-24 × 23-34 µm, verrucose with a conspicuous smooth spot and warts up to 3 µm high (Fig. 31g). Urediospores on *Castilleja* globose-ellipsoid, 14-22 × 17-27 µm, orange, sparsely echinulate, not produced by all races. Teliospores oblong, 12-17 × 30-52 µm, colourless, smooth.

Damage: Mortality may occur as a result of girdling of small diameter stems, and as such can act as a natural thinning agent in young stands. In older trees stem defects occur, reducing wood quality and predisposing trees to damage from wind and heavy snow. *Atropellis piniphila* is often associated with stalactiform blister rust cankers.

Remarks: *Cronartium coleosporioides* can be distinguished from *C. comandrae* by its more elongate cankers, and more precisely by its ellipsoid aeciospores (cf. pear-shaped aeciospores of C. *comandrae*). Differentiating between *C. coleosporioides* and *C. comptoniae* is more difficult. The longitudinal hypertrophied ridges produced by sweet fern blister rust are not present on stems infected by stalactiform blister rust. In addition, the aecial filaments of *C. comptoniae* are continuous, whereas those of *C. coleosporioides* are pendant. Identifying the presence of the alternate hosts will also help distinguish between these two rusts. Non-sporulating cankers may also be confused with those caused by *Atropellis piniphila*.

References:

Peterson, R. S. and F. F. Jewell. 1968. Status of American stem rusts of pine. Ann. Rev. Phytopathol. 6: 23-40.
Ziller, W. G. 1974. The tree rusts of western Canada. Can. For. Serv., Publ. No. 1329. Victoria, B.C.

Figures 31a, 31b: Indian paint brush (31a) and cow wheat (31b), telial hosts of *Cronartium coleosporioides*. Figures 31c, 31d: Aecial pustules on lodgepole pine stems and branches. Figure 31e: Squirrel damage on a sporulating *C. coleosporioides* canker. Figure 31f: Aecial pustules with pendant filaments characteristic of *C. coleosporioides*. Figure 31g: Aeciospores of *C. coleosporioides*.

Comandra Blister Rust

Cronartium comandrae Peck

Basidiomycotina, Uredinales, Cronartiaceae

Hosts: The aecial hosts are 2- and 3- needle hard pines, including lodgepole and ponderosa pine, The telial hosts are Pale Comandra (Fig. 32a) and Bastard toadflax (Fig. 32b).

Distribution: Throughout host range in B.C., but limited to areas where both aecial and telial hosts occur.

Identification: On pines, the rust causes swelling, cracking, and marginal resinosis of bark on stems and branches, forming elongate, sometimes diamond-shaped cankers (Fig. 32c). Perennial cankers grow both vertically and radially, and can girdle stems resulting in the death of tissues distal to the infection. Spermogonial (Fig. 32d) and aecial pustules form within the boundaries of the cankers, producing orange spores in the spring and early summer (Fig. 32e). Uredinia (Fig. 32f) and telia (Fig. 32g) are produced on leaves and stems of the herbaceous alternate hosts in mid- to late-summer.

Microscopic Characteristics: Spermagonia and aecia caulicolous. Spermatia pear-shaped. Aeciospores are orange, finely verrucose, 19-24 × 32-66 µm, with a characteristic pear-shape (Fig. 32h). Urediniospores 20-23 × 22-28 µm, teliospores produced in prominent orange-brown telial columns, 12-15 × 32-44 µm.

Damage: Trees of all sizes and ages are affected, and the presence of cankers can result in growth defects and mortality. Outbreaks of this disease are sporadic, due to variations in the distribution of the alternate host and the periodicity of environmental conditions necessary for infection. The most serious damage has been observed in nurseries and plantations where rapid stem girdling results in high mortality.

Remarks: The aecial cankers of comandra blister rust are very similar in appearance to those of sweet-fern and stalactiform rusts. However, examination of the uniquely shaped aeciospores with a microscope or even a hand-lens will distinguish this rust from others. Swellings on seedlings might be confused with pre-sporulating galls of *Endocronartium harknessii*; however, *C. comandrae* swellings result from swollen bark, while *E. harknessii* galls have normal bark over abnormally thickened xylem tissue.

References:

Hiratsuka, Y. and J. M. Powell. 1976. Pine stem rusts of Canada. Can. For. Serv., NFRC, For. Tech. Rep. 4.

Krebill. R. G. 1968. *Cronartium comandrae* in the Rocky Mountain states. USDA For. Serv., Res. Paper INT-50. Ogden, UT.

Ziller, W. G. 1974. The tree rusts of western Canada. Can. For. Serv., Publ. No. 1329. Victoria, B.C.

Figures 32a, 32b: California comandra (32a) and Bastard toadflax (32b) telial hosts of *Cronartium comandrae*. Figure 32c: Comandra blister rust canker on lodgepole pine in late summer when orange aeciospores are not present. Figure 32d: Droplets of *C. comandrae* spermatia. Figure 32e: Cankers on lodgepole pine with sporulating aecia. Figure 32f: Uredinia on *Comandra umbellata*. 32g: Orange-coloured telial columns on *Comandra umbellata*. Figure 32h: Pear-shaped aeciospore of *Cronartium comandrae*.

Sweetfern Blister Rust

Cronartium comptoniae Arthur

Basidiomycotina, Uredinales, Cronartiaceae

Hosts: *Cronartium comptoniae* is restricted to pines, specifically the two- and three-needle, hard pines. In B.C. it is found on lodgepole, ponderosa, and jack pine in natural forests, and on any of the introduced hard pines including bishop, mugo, Monterey, Scots, and Austrian pines. The alternate (telial) host present in B.C. is sweet gale (Fig. 33a); elsewhere in North America, sweet fern is a host.

Distribution: This fungus has been found throughout the province but is restricted to sites where both pine and sweet gale are present. Sweet gale is found in moist habitats, mainly at low elevations.

Identification: Sweetfern rust first appears as a fusiform swelling on stems and branches of the pine host. The swellings are generally elongate (up to four times longer than broad), diamond-shaped, and often girdle smaller stems and branches. Bark tissue may be thickened resulting in fusiform swelling. During late spring and summer, aecia appear as white-orange blisters that release orange aeciospores (Fig. 33b). During other times of the year, *C. comptoniae* infections may be identified by their size, shape, and by sunken, dead bark and resinosis associated with the cankers. Porcupines and other rodents often preferentially chew on cankers during the winter, leaving exposed wood.

Microscopic Characteristics: Spermatia and aecia on pine caulicolous, spermatia ellipsoid. Aecial filaments on inner surface of peridium continuous (non-stalactiform), extending from the top to the base of the peridia. Aeciospores orange, short-ellipsoid, 16-24 × 24-33 μm, coarsely verrucose with a conspicuous smooth spot and warts up to 3 μm high (Fig. 33c).
   Urediniospores on *Myrica gale* oval-obovate, 16-21 × 23-31 μm, orange-yellow, sparsely echinulate. Teliospores oblong, 13-17 × 28-56 μm, walls faintly coloured, smooth.

Damage: Very little damage has been documented in natural stands, but severe losses have occurred in plantations of susceptible pines located near swampy habitats of sweet fern. Rust cankers are reported as entry points for decay fungi that cause further damage to infected trees.

Remarks: *Cronartium comptoniae* can be distinguished from *C. comandrae* by its ellipsoid aeciospores (cf. pear-shaped aeciospores of *C. comandrae*). Differentiating between *C. comptoniae* and *C. coleosporioides* is more difficult. The aecial filaments of *C. comptoniae* are continuous, whereas those of *C. coleosporioides* are pendant. In addition, longitudinal hypertrophied ridges produced by *C. comptoniae* (Fig. 33d) are not produced on stems infected with *C. coleosporioides*. Identifying the presence of the alternate hosts will also help distinguish between these two rusts.

References:
Anderson, G. W. 1970. Sweetfern rust on hard pines. USDA For. Serv., Pest Leaf. No. 79. Washington, D.C.
Peterson, R. S. and F. F. Jewell. 1968. Status of American stem rusts of pine. Ann. Rev. Phytopathol. 6: 23-40.
Ziller, W. G. 1974. The tree rusts of western Canada. Can. For. Serv., Publ. No. 1329. Victoria, B.C.

Figure 33a: *Myrica gale*, the telial host of *Cronartium comptoniae*. Figure 33b: Aecia of *C. comptoniae* on the main stem and branches of Monterey pine. Figure 33c: Aeciospores of *C. comptoniae*.
Figure 33d: Hypertrophied ridges characteristic of *C. comptoniae* cankers.

White Pine Blister Rust

Cronartium ribicola J. C. Fisch.

Basidiomycotina, Uredinales, Cronartiaceae

Hosts: In B.C., *Cronartium ribicola* affects native five-needle or soft pines, and has been reported on whitebark, sugar, western white, limber, eastern white, and Swiss stone pine (in order of relative susceptibility). Exotic soft pine species planted as ornamentals can also be infected by *C. ribicola*.

The telial hosts include currants and gooseberries (*Ribes* spp.).

Distribution: Five-needle pines are affected throughout their range in B.C., largely in the southern half of the province.

Identification: Infected trees can be identified by the presence of dead branches (red flagging) in the lower portion of the crown. Infections are characterized by diamond-shaped, orange-coloured cankers, evident on young stem and branch tissue with thin, smooth bark (Figs. 34a, 34b). Cankers on older stems have roughened, dead bark, often with resinosis (Fig. 34c). During the spring, white aecial blisters form on the canker, producing orange-coloured aeciospores (Fig. 34d). In the summer, spermatia develop around the margins of the canker in sticky, orangish droplets that dry out and leave small brown scars on the canker surface. Each year, aecia form in the tissue that produced spermatia the previous year.

Infection of *Ribes* spp. (the telial host) occurs shortly after aeciospores are released from pines in the spring. Uredinia appear as yellow-orange pustules on the lower side of leaves (Fig. 34e) in which orange-coloured urediniospores (Fig. 34f) are produced throughout the summer. Opposite the uredinia, on the upper leaf surface, chlorotic-necrotic spots are formed (Fig. 34g). In mid to late summer telial columns form in place of uredinia and appear as brownish-coloured hair-like structures on the lower side of the leaf (Fig. 34h). Heavily infected *Ribes* leaves can appear chlorotic and necrotic, and are sometimes shed prematurely.

Life Cycle:
White pine blister rust alternates between five-needle pines and *Ribes* spp. (currants/gooseberries). Infection takes place through needles in the fall; the fungus grows into and down the branch toward the stem. The fungus grows in the phloem and bark with no visible symptoms for at least three years before spores are produced. In the spring of the 3rd or 4th years, spermatia are formed, followed by the production of aeciospores in white blisters that break through the bark (Fig. 34a). Aeciospores are capable of infecting only *Ribes* spp; approximately 10 days after infection, urediniospore development starts on the leaves and continues throughout the summer (Fig. 34e). Urediniospores are able to reinfect *Ribes* spp., thus intensifying the disease on this host. In the fall, teliospores and basidiospores are produced on *Ribes* spp. that carry the disease back to pine, thereby completing the life cycle.

Microscopic Characteristics: Spermatia and aecia on pine caulicolous, spermatia orange, ellipsoid or ovoid. Aecial filaments on inner surface of peridium lacking or few. Aeciospores orange, short-ellipsoid, 18-20 × 22-31 μm, verrucose with a conspicuous smooth spot and warts up to 2 μm high. Urediospores on *Ribes* spp. hypophyllous, ellipsoid or obovoid, 14-22 × 19-35 μm, sparsely echinulate, orange. Teliospores oblong or cylindric, 8-12 × 30-60 μm, colourless, smooth, forming cinnamon-brown telial columns.

Figure 34a: Aecial pustules of *Cronartium ribicola* on western white pine just before sporulation.
Figure 34b: Sporulating aecia. Figure 34c: *C. ribicola* canker with resinosis in mid-summer, after aeciospore release. Figure 34d: *C. ribicola* aeciospores.

Damage: In many regions of B.C., the volume of white pine has been depleted to the point where it is no longer considered a viable commercial species. The disease is particularly serious in young trees; very few escape infection and many are killed within a few years. Cankers on young trees generally occur within 2.5 m of the ground, due to the presence of susceptible small branches and favourable environmental conditions. Similarly, open-grown trees with persistent branches are more likely to be infected than trees with self-pruned branches growing in dense stands. In older trees, the rust is often confined to isolated branches or the upper crown so that only part of the tree is killed.

Remarks: White pine blister rust is an introduced pathogen, and most natural populations of white pines are highly susceptible. It is believed to have been introduced to British Columbia in 1910 but was not discovered until 1921. It is the only stem rust on white pines and can therefore be easily distinguished from the other similar *Cronartium* rusts on the basis of this host preference. Basal stem cankers producing resin might also be confused with symptoms of Armillaria root rot. The root rot can be distinguished by the presence of white mycelial fans beneath the bark.

References:

Hunt, R. S. 1983. White pine blister rust in British Columbia. Can. For. Serv., Forest Pest Leaf. No. 26. Victoria, B.C.

Ziller, W. G. 1974. The tree rusts of western Canada. Can. For. Serv., Publ. No. 1329. Victoria, B.C.

Figure 34e: *Cronartium ribicola* uredinia on the lower side of a *Ribes* leaf. Figure 34f: *C. ribicola* uredin-iospores. Figure 34g: Chlorotic spots opposite *C. ribicola* uredinia on the upper side of a *Ribes* leaf. Figure 34h: Telial columns of *C. ribicola*.

Western Gall Rust

Endocronartium harknessii (J. P. Moore) Y. Hiratsuka

(= *Peridermium harknessii* J. P. Moore)

Basidiomycotina, Uredinales, Cronartiaceae

Hosts: *Endocronartium harknessii* is restricted to pine, specifically the two-needle, or hard pines. In B.C., it is found on lodgepole, ponderosa, and jack pine in natural forests, and on any of the introduced hard pines including bishop, mugo, Monterey, Scots, and Austrian pines.

Distribution: Western gall rust is widespread throughout the province affecting susceptible trees throughout their range. Because the rust is found in eastern North America as well, the common names "pine-to-pine gall rust" or "globose gall rust" are sometimes used.

Identification: Western gall rust is characterized by the formation of woody swellings (galls) on branches and stems (Fig. 35a). Although the galls are generally globose, they may be asymmetrical and are sometimes deeply fissured. In the late spring (May-July, depending on climate), orange-coloured spores form in blisters beneath the bark of the galls (Fig. 35b). The bark generally sloughs off, exposing spores over much of the gall surface. For most of the year, however, galls are covered with normal bark.

Infection occurs through the succulent tissue of elongating shoots, so all galls are initially formed on one-year-old growth (Fig. 35c). Galls continue to increase in diameter as the host tree grows, and typically reach sizes of 5-10 cm in diameter (although larger galls sometimes develop on main stems). Galls become inactive with the death of the branch or stem, or are often killed by hyperparasitic fungi, but the woody swellings remain on the tree.

Microscopic Characteristics: Spermatia rare, in droplets on gall surface. Aecia and uredinia lacking. Peridermioid teliospores 1-celled, catenulate, oblong, obovate-oblong, or ellipsoid, 14-24 × 23-25 μm, verrucose with tapered columnar rods, wall colourless, spore colour provided by orange lipid bodies within cell, some spores with smooth area on one side (Fig. 35d). Teliospores resemble aeciospores of other *Cronartium* spp.

Damage: Damage is not significant on mature trees where most infections occur on branches. Branch galls do not result in serious growth losses. However, infections on young trees more often result in main stem galls that can cause stem malformations and predispose the tree to breakage in high winds or under heavy snow loads (Figs. 35e, 35f).

Remarks: Unlike the other important stem rusts, *E. harknessii* does not require an alternate host to complete its life cycle. Infection occurs directly from pine-to-pine. This allows rapid intensification of the disease when conditions optimal for infection occur. However, such conditions only occur every several years, resulting in "wave years" of infection and gall formation.

References:

Ziller, W. G. 1974. The tree rusts of western Canada. Can. For. Serv., Publ. No. 1329. Victoria, B.C.

Figure 35a: Branch and stem galls on lodgepole pine caused by *Endocronartium harknessii*. Figure 35b: *E. harknessii* gall with orange spores produced beneath bark. Figure 35c: Immature gall that has never produced spores on one-year old pine branch. Figure 35d: *E. harknessii* spores.
Figure 35e: Main stem galls on nursery-produced pine seedlings. Figure 35f: Stem breakage at the site of a western gall rust gall.

Fir Broom Rust

Melampsorella caryophyllacearum Schroet.
(= *Melampsorella cerastii* (Pers.) Schroet.)

Basidiomycotina, Uredinales, Pucciniastraceae

Hosts: In B.C., the aecial hosts of *Melampsorella caryophyllacearum* are amabilis fir, grand fir, and subalpine fir. Elsewhere in North America it is also found on balsam, noble, California red, Pacific sliver, and white firs. The telial hosts include chickweed, sandwort, and starwort (Fig. 36a).

Distribution: This fungus is widely distributed throughout the range of its hosts in B.C.

Identification: This rust is easily recognized by the conspicuous perennial, systemic brooms formed on branches throughout the crown (Fig. 36b). Infected twigs in the brooms are shorter and thicker than normal (Fig. 36c). At the base of the broom, infected branches and stems are swollen, forming an elongate canker or gall. Stem swellings may be observed after brooms have died and are shed.

Needles in the broom are shorter, thicker, and chlorotic. Spermatia are visible in the spring as orange dots, mainly on the upper surface of needles. Orange-coloured aeciospores are produced in pustules on the lower surfaces of needles, giving the entire broom a yellow-orange appearance during sporulation (Fig. 36d). The needles die and are shed in the fall (Fig. 36e).

Uredinia develop on both sides of alternate host leaves, appearing as orange-red pustules, producing yellow-orange urediniospores. Teliospores on the lower epidermis give leaves and orange cast. The rust is systemic on perennial alternate hosts, and can therefore persist in the absence of the fir host.

Microscopic Characteristics: Aeciospores orange, globose, finely verrucose, 14-18 × 16-28 μm. Urediniospores yellow-orange, ellipsoid, sparsely echinulate, 12-18 × 16-30 μm. Telia on lower leaf surfaces, teliospores within lower epidermis, single-celled, cylindric, 13-20 μm wide.

Damage: Fir broom rust has not caused serious damage in B.C., but elsewhere in North America, and in Europe severe growth loss and mortality have been reported.

Remarks: This fungus is systemic and perennial on both aecial and telial hosts. As a result, the rust may be found in areas where one of the hosts is not present. The brooming symptoms on true firs caused by *M. caryophyllacearum* could be confused with mistletoe infections or brooms caused by physiological abnormalities. However, the chlorotic needles in the summer and complete loss of needles in the winter are diagnostic features of the rust.

References:
Peterson, R. S. 1964. Fir broom rust. USDA For. Serv., Pest Leaf. No. 87. Washington, D.C.
Ziller, W. G. 1974. The tree rusts of western Canada. Can. For. Serv., Publ. No. 1329. Victoria, B.C.

Figure 36a: Crisp sandwort, one of the telial hosts of *Melampsorella caryophyllacearum*.

Figures 36b, 36c: Brooming symptoms associated with *M. caryophyllacearum*. Figure 36d: Aecia on lower needle surfaces. Figure 36e: Fir broom symptom during the winter months with no needles.

Hemlock - Blueberry Rust

Naohidemyces vaccinii (Wint.) Sato, Katsuya & Hiratsuka
(= *Pucciniastrum vaccinii* (Wint.) Joerst.)
(= *Pucciniastrum myrtilli* Arthur)

Basidiomycotina, Uredinales, Pucciniastraceae

Hosts: In B.C., the aecial hosts of *Naohidemyces vaccinii* are western, mountain, and eastern hemlock. The telial hosts in B.C. include black huckleberry, dwarf bilberry, grouseberry, evergreen huckleberry, he-huckleberry, lignonberry, little-leaf huckleberry, oval-leaf blueberry, red huckleberry, and velvet-leaf blueberry,

Distribution: This fungus is widely distributed throughout the range of its hosts in B.C.

Identification: The infected needles of hemlock become chlorotic or discoloured and may be shed prematurely (Figs. 37a, 37b). Diseased trees therefore show symptoms of needle necrosis and thinning foliage. Yellow-orange aeciospores are produced in shallow-conical aecial pustules that develop in rows on the lower surface of needles (Fig. 37c).

Uredinia are produced on the lower surface of leaves on the alternate host, appearing as pustules which produce yellow-orange urediniospores (Fig. 37d). In late summer, telia form as flat, dark-coloured crusts on lower leaf surfaces.

Microscopic Characteristics: Spermogonia hypophyllous, subcuticular, without bounding structure, 80-150 μm in diameter and up to 70 μm in height. Aecia on current years needles rarely on cone scales, hypophyllous, in two rows divided by midrib of needle, 200-400 μm in diameter, 100-200 μm in height, subepidermal in origin, dome-like, peridium with many hemi-spherical differentiated ostiolar cells 10-14 μm in diameter. Aeciospores globose to sub-globose, often narrower at the bottom, conspicuously echinulate (Fig. 37e), borne singly on pedicels, 19.5-29 × 14-19.5 μm, yellow. Uredinia hypophyllous, up to 500 μm in diameter or sometimes several coalescing, dome-shaped, peridium with conspicuous ostiolar cells (14)16.5-43 × 7.5-17.5 μm. Urediniospores subglobose, echinulate, 17.5-27.5 × 10-19 μm (Fig. 37f). Teliospores one spore deep, consisting of several laterally adherent cells within epidermal cells, 20-30 × 18-23 μm in surface view, 16-22 mm in height, one germ pore in the centre of each cell, wall lightly pigmented.

Damage: Damage to either host is negligible and localized in areas where hemlock regeneration grows intermingled with huckleberries and blueberries.

Remarks: Until recently, this rust was considered a part of the genus *Pucciniastrum*. However, because of the unique structure of its aecia, it has been placed in the genus *Naohidemyces*. Another needle rust, *Melampsora epitea,* which is also found on hemlock could be confused with *N. vaccinii*. The aecia of *M. epitea* are "loose," with no peridium covering the aeciospores, while those of *N. vaccinii* have a dome-shaped covering with a centrally located hole (ostiole) through which spores are released.

References:
Sato, S., K. Katsuya, and Y. Hiratsuka. 1993. Morphology, taxonomy and nomenclature of *Tsuga*-Ericaceae rusts. Trans. Mycol. Soc. Japan 34: 47-62.

Ziller, W. G. 1974. The tree rusts of western Canada. Can. For. Serv., Publ. No. 1329. Victoria, B.C.

Figure 37a, 37b: Discoloured hemlock needles resulting from *Naohidemyces vaccinii* infection (37a: upper needle surfaces, 37b: lower needle surfaces). 37c: Aecia on the lower surface of hemlock needles. Figure 37d: Uredinia on *Vaccinium*. Figure 37e: Echinulate aeciospores of *N. vaccinii* and dome-shaped aecium. Figure 37f: Echinulate urediniospores.

Fir - Fireweed Rust

Pucciniastrum epilobii G. Otth.

(= *Pucciniastrum fuchsiae* Hiratsuka)

Basidiomycotina, Uredinales, Pucciniastraceae

Hosts: In B.C., the aecial hosts of *Pucciniastrum epilobii* are amabilis fir, white fir, and subalpine fir. Elsewhere in North America it is also reported on grand fir and balsam fir.

The alternate (telial) hosts in B.C. include several species of fireweed (Fig. 38a), godetia, and fuschia.

Distribution: This fungus is widely distributed throughout the range of its hosts in B.C.

Identification: The infected needles of fir become chlorotic or discoloured and may be shed prematurely. Consequently, infected trees show symptoms of needle necrosis and thinning foliage. Spermagonia appear in the spring as small black dots on the lower surface of new needles. These are followed by cylindrical aecial pustules on the lower surface of current years needles (Fig. 38b). After aeciospore discharge in early summer, aecia persist until needles die and are shed. Uredinia are produced on the lower surface of leaves on the alternate host, appearing as pustules that produce yellow-orange urediniospores (Fig. 38c). In late summer, telia form as flat, dark-coloured crusts on lower leaf surfaces.

Microscopic Characteristics: Aecia on current years needles or cone scales hypophyllous, peridermioid, cylindric-flat cylindric, 0.12-0.03 mm in diameter; and ≈1.0 mm high, aeciospores yellow, catenulate, finely verrucose, 15 × 19 µm, with an elongate smooth spot.

Urediniospores with orange-yellow contents, sparsely and finely echinulate, 13-18 × 17-24 µm; telia hypophyllous, subepidermal, dark coloured.

Damage: Damage to fir varies from year-to-year, depending on local environmental conditions and the proximity of the alternate host. Serious levels of defoliation and mortality have occurred in young stands growing in recently logged areas where fireweed is abundant.

Remarks: A number of other needle rusts are found on fir that could be confused with *P. epilobii*. These include:

fir - blueberry rust	*Pucciniastrum goeppertianum* (Kühn) Kleb.
common fir - bracken rust	*Uredinopsis pteridis* Dietel & Holw. in Dietel
Hashioka's fir - bracken rust	*Uredinopsis hashiokai* Hiratsuka
fir - ladyfern rust	*Uredinopsis longimucronata* Faull
fir - willow rust	*Melampsora abieti-capraearum* Tub.

These rusts are superficially similar, but can be differentiated by careful examination of aecia shape, aeciospore colour, and the location of foliar damage.

Pucciniastrum epilobii can become perennial in fireweed, overwintering in the roots, and reinfecting leaves as they develop the following year.

References:

Bauman, N. G. and E. Wegwitz. 1972. Needle rusts of the true firs in British Columbia. Can. For. Serv., Forest Pest Leaf. No. 45. Victoria, B.C.

Ziller, W. G. 1974. The tree rusts of western Canada. Can. For. Serv., Publ. No. 1329. Victoria, B.C.

Figure 38a: Fireweed, the most common telial host of *Pucciniastrum epilobii*. Figure 38b: Aecia on subalpine fir needles. Figure 38c: Uredinia of *P. epilobii* on the lower surface of a fireweed leaf.

Atropellis Canker

Atropellis piniphila (Weir) Lohman & Cash

Ascomycotina, Helotiales, Helotiaceae

Hosts: *Atropellis piniphila* is found only on pine. In B.C., it has been reported on **lodgepole** and ponderosa pine. Elsewhere in North America it has also been found on jack, loblolly, shortleaf, Virginia, and whitebark pines.

Distribution: Atropellis canker is common throughout the southern two thirds of the province, but has not been reported north of a line extending from Hazelton to Fort St. John.

Identification: Perennial cankers form on branches and stems of lodgepole pine causing resinosis, distortion in growth, and a blue-black stain of the sapwood and heartwood (Figs. 39a, 39b). Infection generally occurs through undamaged bark near branch nodes on stems 15-30 years old. Cankers, which are usually centered around a branch stub, increase in size by approximately 5 cm in length and 0.6 cm in circumference annually, and can reach 3 m in length. Two types of fruiting bodies, pycnidia and apothecia, are often present. Pycnidia usually appear on young cankers, before apothecia, are globose, 0.6-1.6 mm across when wet, and produce conidia in a creamy mucilaginous mass when wet. Apothecia are stalked, black saucer-like structures, 0.6-4.5 mm in diameter, which form singly or in groups in the center of the canker and are present throughout the year (Figs. 39c, 39d). Ascospores are produced by apothecia and are disseminated by wind for distances up to 100 m.

Although other stem disorders result in resinous cankers, *A. piniphila* is readily distinguished by the blue-black staining of the sapwood (and to a lesser extent, the heartwood) underlying the canker (39d, 39e). The sapwood at the leading edge of the canker is stained a reddish-brown colour.

Microscopic Characteristics: Apothecial tissue colours 5% KOH bluish-green. Hymenium purplish in cross section. Asci clavate, 8-spored, IKI-, 90-160 × 10-15 µm. Ascospores ellipsoid-fuscoid, hyaline, 0-1 septate, 16-28 × 4-7 µm. Paraphyses filiform, septate, branched. Conidiophores verticulate, 30-65 µm long, terminating in a phialide, 30-40 µm long. Conidia rod-shaped, nonseptate, hyaline, 4-8 × 1-1.7 µm.

Damage: Damage occurs as mortality, growth reduction, and reduction of value for both chips and finished wood products. The high resin content also interferes with penetration by wood preservatives. Mortality occurs when stems are girdled by large or multiple cankers, and may be severe in dense stands, particularly those growing on dry sites.

Remarks: Trees less than 15 yrs old rarely become infected. In older trees, most infections occur on tissues that are 10-30 yrs old at the time of infection. Virtually no infections occur on tissues less than 5 yrs or greater than 40 yrs old. High levels of infection have been observed after fire in lodgepole pine regeneration that are infected by diseased residual trees not killed in the fire. A closely related fungus, *Atropellis pinicola* Zeller & Good. is less commonly found in B.C. This fungus attacks branches of western white pine, and occasionally, lodgepole pine.

References:

Baranyay, J. A., T. Szabo, and K. Hunt. 1973. Effect of Atropellis canker on growth and utilization of lodgepole pine. Can. For. Serv., Inf. Rep. BC-X-86.

Hopkins, J. C. 1963. Atropellis canker of lodgepole pine: etiology, symptoms, and canker development rates. Can. J. Bot. 41:1536-1545.

Hopkins, J. C. and B. Callan. 1991. Atropellis canker. Can. For. Serv., Forest Pest Leaf. No. 25. Victoria, B.C.

Figures 39a, 39b: Cankers caused by *Atropellis piniphila* on lodgepole pine. Figure 39c: Canker on young lodgepole pine showing apothecia and blue stain in sapwood. Figure 39d: *A. piniphilia* apothecia.
Figure 39e: Blue staining of sapwood that follows annual growth rings.

Cytospora Canker

Cytospora chrysosperma (Pers.:Fr.) Fr.

(= *Cytospora pulcherrima* Dearn. & Hansbrough)

Deuteromycotina, Coelomycetes, Sphaeropsidales, Sphaeropsidaceae

(teleomorph = *Valsa sordida* Nitschke)

Ascomycotina, Diaporthales, Valsaceae

Hosts: In B.C., *Cytospora chrysosperma* has been reported on maple, **cottonwood**, **trembling aspen**, **lombardy poplar**, and **willow**. Elsewhere in North America it has also been found on paper and water birch, apple, white poplar, chokecherry, oak, elderberry, and mountain-ash. It is likely that all willow and poplar species are susceptible to this fungus.

Distribution: This fungus is widely distributed throughout the range of its hosts in B.C. It is common throughout the northern hemisphere and Australia, and is likely to accompany imported host plant material.

Identification: The disease occurs on stems, branches, and twigs, forming elongate cankers, regular or irregular in outline, generally with defined borders (Figs. 40a, 40b). Cankers appear as discoloured sunken zones, with a slightly raised perimeter formed by annual callus growth. The inner bark of diseased tissue turns brown to black and may have a distinct foul odour. The sapwood associated with cankers is light to reddish brown. Several years after infection, dead bark lifts away from the stem and falls off. Fruiting bodies (pycnidial stromata) of the asexual stage of the fungus (*Cytospora*) form within the cankers, just beneath the cuticle of the dead bark, appearing as short grey-black cones, 0.5-1 mm in diameter. Sticky masses of conidia ooze out of the pycnidia forming long, orange-red, coiled "spore tendrils" (Fig. 40c). Perithecia of the sexual stage (*Valsa*) are more rare. They appear as spherical black structures beneath the bark in clusters of 6-12, each ≈0.5 mm in diameter.

Microscopic Characteristics: Stromata conic to truncate-conic, 0.5-2 mm diameter, breaking through the bark to expose a prominent dark grey disc (ectostroma). Perithecia embedded in the bark, 6-12 in a cluster, globose to compressed, 300-500 µm diameter, dark brown; ostiolar necks collectively erumpent through ectostroma, 500-700 µm long. Asci clavate, with apical ring, 8-spored, 30-45 × 5-7 µm; ascospores hyaline, allantoid, unicellular, both ends rounded, 7-12 × 1.5-2.5 µm. Pycnidial stroma immersed in the bark, 0.5-1.5 mm diameter, multilocular, ostiole erumpent, wall indistinct. Conidiophores usually branched, hyaline, phialidic, 10-40 mm long. Conidia hyaline, allantoid, unicellular, 3-5 × 1-1.5 µm, often emerging in long orange tendrils.

Damage: This disease is rarely a problem of economic importance in natural stands, but can cause serious damage in forest nurseries, young plantations, and in horticultural settings.

Remarks: *Cytospora chrysosperma* has been shown to inhabit healthy bark of aspen and beech, causing disease only in trees or branches of low vigour or when the hosts are stressed by drought, injury, sunscald, fire, or other pathological disorders. The presence of this disease generally indicates that the trees are under stress.

References:

Bloomberg, W J. 1962. Cytospora canker on poplar. Can. J. Bot. 40:1271-1292.

Chapela, I. H. 1989. Fungi in healthy stems and branches of American beech and aspen: a comparative study. New Phytologist 113: 64-75.

Figures 40a, 40b: Cankers caused by *Cytospora chrysosperma* on trembling aspen.
Figure 40c: Spore tendrils of *C. chrysosperma* on trembling aspen.

Phomopsis Canker of Douglas-fir

Diaporthe lokoyae Funk
(anamorph =*Phomopsis lokoyae* Hahn)

Ascomycotina, Diaporthales, Valsaceae

Hosts: In B.C., *Diaporthe lokoyae* has been reported on western larch, Sitka spruce, western red-cedar, western hemlock, **Douglas-fir**, and dawn redwood.

Distribution: Phomopsis canker is widespread throughout the range of coastal Douglas-fir; most records of this disease are from the coastal regions, predominantly southern Vancouver Island and the lower mainland. One collection has been confirmed in the interior of the province, near Vernon.

Identification: Leader and branch dieback occurs associated with cankers on diseased seedlings and young trees. Cankers appear as brown, sunken, elliptical areas of dead bark with a well defined margin. They are often centered around a dead twig or branch, or are associated with dieback of growing shoots (Fig. 41). Fruiting bodies of both the sexual stage (*Diaporthe*), and the

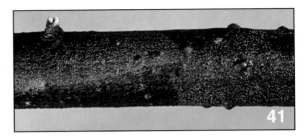

Figure 41: Phomopsis canker on Douglas-fir.

asexual stage (*Phomopsis*) form on the surface of the cankered bark as small (≈0.5 mm in diameter), dark-coloured pimples. Both types of fruiting bodies may be found throughout the year.

Microscopic Characteristics: Perithecia in clusters of 2-4, black, subglobose, 300-400 μm diameter; ostioles cylindric, 100-270 μm long. Asci cylindric, 8-spored, 36-68 × 7-12 μm with apical refractive ring. Ascospores cylindric-ellipsoid, constricted at a single septum, terminal appendages at each end, hyaline, 10-16 × 2.5-4.5 μm, each cell containing two oil drops. Paraphyses broad and tapering, up to 200 μm long, 8-10 μm wide at the base, 3-4 μm wide at the rounded tip, hyaline, simple or branched, septate.

Pycnidia erumpent, black, lenticular to subglobose, 300-600 μm in diameter, 200-300 μm high. Conidiophores lining the single locule, flexuous, subulate, 5-20 μm long; conidiogenous cells phialidic. Conidia of two types: a-spores hyaline, elliptic-fusoid, non-septate, containing two oil droplets, 6-10 × 2-4 μm; ß-spores hyaline, elongate-fusiform, nonseptate, minutely guttulate, 10-12 × 1.5-2.5 μm.

Damage: Sporadic outbreaks of this disease occur in plantations and nurseries. Most damage is minor, particularly on older trees. Severe top-kill and girdling of younger trees can result in poor growth form or mortality.

Remarks: This disease is known as Phomopsis canker because the asexual stage is more common, and was described prior to the discovery of the sexual stage (*Diaporthe*).

References:
Funk, A. 1968. *Diaporthe lokoyae* n. sp., the perfect state of *Phomopsis lokoyae*. Can. J. Bot. 46: 601-603.

Rough Bark of Alder

Didymosphaeria oregonensis Goodd.

Ascomycotina, Dothideales, Didymosphaeriaceae

Hosts: *Didymosphaeria oregonensis* has been only been found on alder. In B.C., it has been reported on Sitka, mountain, and red alder.

Distribution: This fungus is widely distributed throughout the range of its hosts in B.C.

Identification: Spindle-shaped cankers are common on stems and branches of young alder trees. At the site of a canker, the stem is often swollen, with a band of rough bark encircling the stem (Fig. 42). Bands of rough bark range from 1-60 cm in length.

Microscopic Characteristics: Pseudothecia black, globose, ostiolate, pseudoparenchymatous, 1 mm in diameter, immersed, single. Asci bitunicate, cylindric-clavate, 8-spored, 75-90 μm long. Ascospores greenish, ellipsoid, 1-septate, 18-21 × 7-9 μm. Pseudoparaphyses filiform, branched, septate.

Damage: The presence of this fungus appears to have little effect on the health or productivity of alder trees. Young trees are occasionally deformed and/or stunted when numerous cankers are present.

Remarks: The infection of alder by *Didymosphaeria oregonensis* is thought to be restricted to young trees, and the cankers cease to grow after the bark thickens with age. The rough bark remains, however, on the trunks of mature trees.

References:

Gooding, L. N. 1931. *Didymosphaeria oregonensis*, a new canker organism on alder. Phytopathology 21: 913-918.

Figure 42: Canker caused by *Didymosphaeria oregonensis* on red alder.

Hypoxylon Canker

Entoleuca mammata (Wahlenberg) J. D. Rogers & Y. M. Ju
Hypoxylon mammatum (Wahlenberg) P. Karst.

(= *Hypoxylon pruinatum* (Klotzch) Cke.)

Ascomycotina, Sphaeriales, Xylariaceae

Hosts: *Hypoxylon mammatum* is found only on hardwoods, most commonly on **poplar** and willow. In B.C., it has been reported on aspen, willow, and Sitka alder. Elsewhere in North America it has also been found on other poplar spp., birch, apple, oak, and hophornbeam.

Distribution: Hypoxylon canker is reported with low frequency from all parts of the province.

Identification: Hypoxylon cankers first appear as sunken, yellow-orange areas on the bark of stems, centered around dead branch stubs or injuries. The bark associated with older cankers becomes mottled, then necrotic with small blisters of dead bark appearing at the canker margins (Fig. 43a). Cankers enlarge rapidly attaining lengths > 1 m, and often girdle the stems. Hyphal pegs, or pillars, bearing conidia form beneath dead bark, pushing it away from the underlying cortical tissues. Two to three years after the initial infection, perithecia form on the surface of the canker. The perithecia are embedded in stromata and have a prominent nipple-like tip through which ascospores are released (42b, 43c). The perithecial stroma is fertile for only 1 year but may persist for several years. It is greyish at first, and becomes black with age.

Microscopic Characteristics: Ascostromata immersed or erumpent, discrete, whitish pruinose at first, becoming black, 2-5 mm in diameter, 1-2 mm thick, usually coalescing to form effused stromata up to 25 mm in length, smooth except for papillate ostioles, carbonaceous, sometimes tuberculate; perithecia globose, single or up to 30 in a stroma, 0.7-1 mm in diameter; asci cylindric, with J+ apical plugs, 140-200 × 12-16 μm with stipe 30-40 μm long; ascospores uniseriate, ellipsoid, dark brown, with a germination slit running along the axis of the spore, 20-30 × 9-12 μm. Paraphyses present but indistinct and gelatinizing. Conidial state: Grey, pillar-like hyphal pegs arising from a brownish subiculum below the periderm. Conidiophores branched, with 2-3 terminal conidiogenous branches, 75-150 μm high. Conidia developing on geniculations on conidiogenous branches, hyaline, ellipsoid, 6-9 × 2-4 μm.

Damage: Trees with main stem cankers usually die within 5 years or are structurally weakened and break in the wind. Most damage occurs on injured or stressed trees, and on trees growing in poorly stocked or open stands. In some regions of the eastern USA, annual losses are estimated to be 30% of the net growth of aspen.

Remarks: Although *H. mammatum* has been recorded throughout British Columbia, the incidence and loss to the disease are low. In contrast, the fungus is commonly found on aspen in Alberta. The factors contributing to infection by *H. mammatum* appear to be very complex and it is difficult to predict where and when disease will occur. There does seem to be variation in both susceptibility among poplar clones, and virulence of the fungus. Cankers caused by *H. mammatum* could be confused with other cankers or bark anomalies, but the presence of hyphal pegs and perithecia are unique diagnostic features.

References:

Anderson, R. L. and G. W. Anderson. 1969. Hypoxylon canker of aspen. USDA For. Serv., Pest Leaf. No. 6. Washington, D.C.

Rogers, J. D. 1979. The Xylariaceae: systematic, biological and evolutionary aspects. Mycologia 71: 1-43.

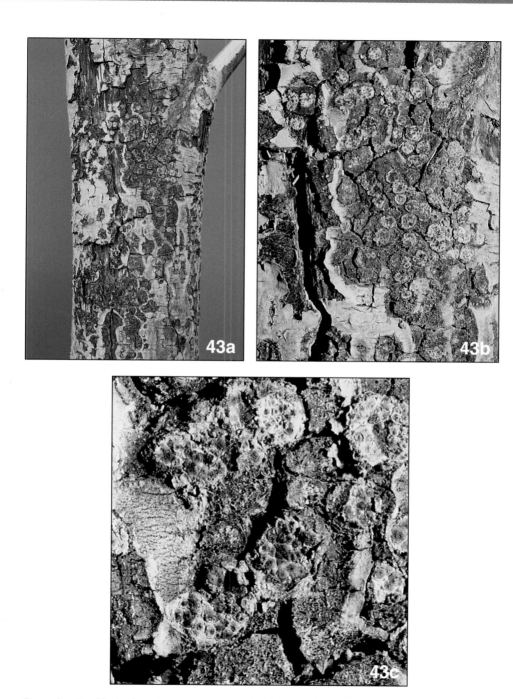

Figure 43a: Dead bark of trembling aspen associated with Hypoxylon canker.
Figures 43b, 43c: Perithecia embedded in stroma.

Sterile Conk Trunk Rot of Birch

Inonotus obliquus (Pers.:Fr.) Pilát

(= *Polyporus obliquus* (Pers.:Fr.) Fr.)
(= *Poria obliqua* (Pers.:Fr.) P. Karst.)

Basidiomycotina, Aphyllophorales, Polyporaceae

Hosts: In B.C., *Inonotus obliquus* has been reported on **paper birch** and rarely on cottonwood. Elsewhere in North America it has also been found on alder, hickory, beech, and *Ostrya* (American leverwood or hophornbeam).

Distribution: This fungus is widely distributed throughout the range of its hosts in B.C.

Identification: The most prominent character used to identify this fungus is the presence of "sterile conks." These are conspicuous perennial black masses of fungal tissue, commonly 20-30 cm in diameter, that erupt from bark cankers (Fig. 44a). The conk surface is rough and cracked, and the internal tissue of the conk is yellow-brown to rust-brown, with a punky texture (Fig. 44b). The tree trunk is often thickened at the site of the conk, a result of increased wood production and thicker bark. In contrast, fertile fruiting bodies are less conspicuous and annual, forming in the summer and early fall under the bark or outer layers of wood surrounding sterile conks on dead standing or fallen trees. As the sporophores develop, the bark and outermost wood rings split and lift away exposing the spore-bearing surface. The fertile sporophores quickly deteriorate through insect and weather damage and are usually difficult to find. The fruiting body is resupinate, 1-3 mm thick, with a grey to reddish-brown pore surface. Pores appear as oblique openings to vertically aligned tubes, 6-8 per mm.

Incipient decay is yellowish white in irregular zones. Advanced decay occurs in the heartwood, moving to the sapwood after trees die, and appears in alternating zones of white and light reddish-brown wood. White veins of mycelium are common near the cankers. Dark zone lines are often present throughout the decayed wood (Fig. 44c).

Microscopic Characteristics: Hyphae in the context of the fruiting body thin- to moderately thick-walled, frequently branched, simple septate, basidiospores broadly ellipsoid to ovoid, hyaline to pale brownish, IKI-, 9-10 × 5.5-6.5 μm. Growth in culture slow, mat white becoming yellow to brown, hyphae hyaline, thin-walled, simple septate, thick-walled setae, laccase positive. Stalpers: 1 3 (4) (9) (10) (11) (12) (13) (14) 17 21 22 25 (26) 30 (31) (34) 35 (38) 48 52 53 67 69 (70) 83 (88) 89.

Damage: Infected trees are severely damaged. The presence of a single sterile conk indicates extensive heartwood decay; 50-100% cull is assumed.

Remarks: Infection occurs through dead branch stubs, trunk wounds, or through pre-existing cankers (e.g., *Nectria*) by spores produced by fertile fruiting bodies. Decay characteristics and small sterile conks are similar in appearance to those of *Phellinus igniarius*.

References:

Campbell, W. A. and R. W. Davidson. 1938. A *Poria* as the fruiting stage of the fungus causing the sterile conks on birch. Mycologia 30: 553-560.

True, R. P., E. H. Tyron, and J. F. King. 1955. Cankers and decays of birch associated with two *Poria* species. J. For. 53: 412-415.

Zabel, R. A. 1976. Basidiocarp development in *Inonotus obliquus* and its inhibition by stem treatments. For. Sci. 22: 431-437.

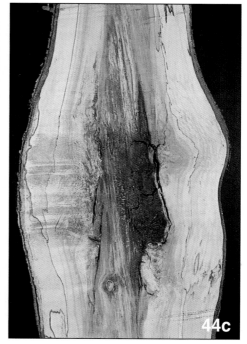

Figure 44a: A sterile conk of *Inonotus obliquus* on paper birch.

Figure 44b: The yellow-brown colour of the context of a sterile conk of *I. obliquus*.

Figure 44c: Advanced decay in paper birch caused by *I. obliquus*.

Nectria Canker

Nectria cinnabarina (Tode ex Fr.) Fr.
(anamorph = *Tubercularia vulgaris* Tode ex Fr.)

Ascomycotina, Hypocreales, Hypocreaceae

Distribution: *Nectria cinnabarina* is widely distributed throughout the range of its hosts in B.C.

Hosts: Species of *Nectria* that cause cankers and dieback are common on a wide range of hosts, mostly hardwoods. In B.C., *N. cinnabarina* has been found on vine and bigleaf maple, horse chestnut, mimosa, red alder, saskatoon, quince, *Choisya*, Pacific dogwood, hazelnut, *Cotoneaster*, fig, honey locust, apple, plum, cherry, pear, buckthorn, blackberry, willow, mountain ash, *Spiraea*, western hemlock, and elm. The reader is referred to Farr *et al.* (1989) for the extensive listing of *N. cinnabarina* hosts elsewhere in North America.

Identification: The initial symptoms of infection generally appear in the spring with sudden wilting of leaves or the failure of leaves to appear. Sunken cankers are generally associated with wounds or at the bases of dying branches, and may girdle branches or small stems. Bark within cankers dies and appears dry and cracked.

The most prominent sign of infection is the presence of masses of orange-pink coloured "coral-spots" for which the disease is named (Fig. 45a). These are conidia-producing fruiting structures, called sporodochia, which develop through cracks or natural openings in the cankered bark in the spring and early summer. They range in size from 0.5-1.5 mm in diameter and height. Young sporodochia are pink-orange to purplish-red when young, and become tan-to-brown or black as they mature. Later in the summer, orange-red coloured sexual fruiting structures, perithecia, form in groups around sporodochia. Perithecia are globose, approximately 0.4 mm in diameter, with a rough outer wall (Fig. 45b).

Microscopic Characteristics: Perithecia red, clustered on the top edge of an erumpent conidial stroma, globose, slightly collapsed at the ostiole, rough outer wall, ≈400 µm in diameter. Asci cylindric clavate, 8-spored, 60-90 × 9-14 µm. Ascospores elliptic-cylindric, hyaline, slightly constricted at the single, central septum, 12-20 × 4-9 µm. Sporodochia pink to light red, erumpent through the bark, cushion-shaped, up to 3 mm in diameter. Phialides subulate, 20-30 × 2-4 µm, arising from the pseudoparenchymatic stroma, densely packed. Conidia oval to cylindric, 5-7 × 2-3 µm, produced in large masses and supported in a mucous matrix.

Damage: *Nectria cinnabarina* acts mostly as a saprophyte, living on dead plant tissue, and as such is not generally considered a serious forest disease organism. However, it is also weakly pathogenic, colonizing stems and branches weakened by mechanical injury, physiological stress, or other disease. Damage by this fungus is often observed on recently transplanted ornamental shrubs and trees.

Remarks: Two other related *Nectria* species cause notable cankers on hardwoods, but occur much less frequently in B.C.: *N. galligena* Bres. in Strauss causes perennial "target" cankers on many hardwoods and fruit trees (European canker) (Fig. 45c), and *N. ditissima* Tul. causes large perennial stem cankers on red alder (Fig. 45d). Isolates of *N. ditissima* are being considered as biological control agents for red alder.

References:
Funk, A. 1981. Parasitic microfungi of western trees. Can. For. Serv., Rep. BC-X-222.

Figures 45a, 45b: Sporodochia (45a) and perithecia (45b) of *Nectria cinnabarina*. Figure 45c: "Target" canker caused by *N. galligena*. Figure 45d: A perennial canker on red alder caused by *N. ditissima*.

Silver Leaf Disease

Chondrostereum purpureum (Pers.:Fr.) Pouzar

(= *Stereum purpureum* Pers.:Fr.)

Basidiomycotina, Aphyllophorales, Stereaceae

Hosts: *Chondrostereum purpureum* is very commonly found on angiosperms, less so on conifers. In B.C., it has been reported on red and mountain alder, paper birch, apple, trembling aspen, balsam and black poplar, horsechestnut, maple, most *Prunus* spp., willow, subalpine fir, white spruce, Douglas-fir, western redcedar, and western hemlock. Elsewhere in North America it has also been found on grand and amabilis fir, *Amelanchier, Arbutus, Cotoneaster,* hornbeam, hickory, hackberry, dogwood, quince, beech, tulip-tree, mountain ash, tupelo, *Ostrya*, London plane-tree, pear, oak, lilac, elm, and grape.

Distribution: This fungus is widely distributed throughout the range of its hosts in B.C.

Identification: The common name "silver leaf disease" refers to the silver or leaden luster of leaves that occurs on some hosts (e.g., apple and *Prunus* spp.) resulting from air spaces that form between epidermal and palisade cells. Affected leaves become brown at midribs and margins. Fruiting bodies are common on the dead wood of standing and fallen broadleaved trees, and on cut surfaces of slash. They are annual (often persisting from year-to-year), resupinate to semi-pileate, extending out 2-4 cm from the substrate, and often form in groups (Figs. 46a, 46b). The upper surface of the sporophore is tomentose, greyish-white to purple, indistinctly zoned with a light-coloured margin. The hymenial surface is smooth or slightly wrinkled, bright purple when fresh, brown-violet when old. Fruiting bodies are 1-2.5 mm thick with a black line visible in cross section.

The incipient stage of decay appears as a reddish-brown stain (Fig. 46c). As decay advances the stain disappears and the wood becomes bleached. In final stages of decay wood is dry, light in weight, and white-mottled to pale yellow in colour.

Microscopic Characteristics: Hyphae in fruiting body thin- to thick-walled, 2.5-4 µm in diameter, clamps. Basidiospores elliptical to cylindrical, hyaline, smooth, non-amyloid, 6.5-8 × 2.5-3.5 µm Growth in culture rapid, mat white to light buff, ovoid terminal vesicles, laccase positive. Stalpers: 1 3 (5) (6) 13 14 (15) 17 19 21 23 25 30 31 (37) 39 or (39) (42) 45 48 51 52 53 54 (60) 75 (82) 83 (88) 89 (94) 95 97 99.

Damage: The economic impact of the disease is greater on ornamental and orchard trees than on trees in a forestry setting. *Chondrostereum purpureum* is largely a saprophyte but can be a weak parasite on living hardwoods. Toxins produced by the fungus affect leaves, and on some hosts kill branches or entire trees. This fungus is currently being considered as a candidate for use as a biocontrol agent for hardwood stump sprouts.

Remarks: Other related fungi in the Stereaceae such as *Amylostereum, Stereum, Columnocystis* or *Peniophora* could be confused with old fruiting bodies of *C. purpureum*.

References:

Thomas, G. P. and D. G. Podmore. 1953. Studies in forest pathology. XI Decay in black cottonwood in the middle Fraser region, British Columbia. Can. J. Bot. 31: 675-692.

Wall, R. E. 1990. The fungus *Chondrostereum purpureum* as a silvicide to control stump sprouting in hardwoods. North. J. Appl. For. 7:17-19.

Figures 46a, 46b: Fruiting bodies of *Chondrostereum purpureum*.
Figure 46c: Stain associated with decay.

Grey-Brown Sap Rot

Cryptoporus volvatus (Peck) Shear

(= *Polyporus volvatus* Peck)

Basidiomycotina, Aphyllophorales, Polyporaceae

Hosts: Grey sap rot has been reported from a wide range of coniferous hosts but is most common in bark beetle- and fire-killed **Douglas-fir**. In B.C., the fungus has been reported on amabilis, grand, and subalpine fir, Sitka and white spruce, lodgepole, ponderosa and western white pine, Douglas-fir, and western hemlock. Elsewhere in North America it has also been found on black and Englemann spruce, California incense cedar, and western larch.

Distribution: This fungus is widely distributed throughout the range of its hosts in B.C.

Identification: The fruiting bodies are annual, leathery, pouch-like structures, up to 4 cm wide × 5 cm high × 4 cm deep (Figs. 47a, 47b). The upper surface is smooth, and yellow to light brown turning white with age. The brown poroid lower surface is at first covered with a hard membrane continuous with the upper surface, hence the common name "pouch fungus." Later an opening forms at the base of the membrane to permit the release of the spores.

The fungus causes a cream to light grey discoloration in narrow bands in the outer sapwood; the discoloration is particularly evident in a radial or tangential section. In the advanced stage, the affected wood is light brown, cubical and crumbly.

Microscopic Characteristics: Hyphae in the context of the fruiting body are thin-walled with clamps at all septae. Basidiospores cylindric, hyaline, smooth, IKI-, 12-16.5 x 4.5 µm. Growth in culture moderate to slow, mat white, odour pungent, laccase positive. Stalpers: 1 3 (7) (9) (11) 13 (14) (16) (17) (18) 30 (36) 39 42 44 45 (47) 52 53 (54) (79) 80 90 (94).

Damage: Grey sap rot develops rapidly in dead standing trees but is quite superficial, limited to the outer 1-2 cm of sapwood. As a result, little or no board-foot volume loss is associated with this decay.

Remarks: Fruiting bodies usually develop the year after tree death occurs, and often form by the hundreds up the stem (Fig. 47c). Top breakage sometimes occurs as a result of decay several years after infection by *Cryptoporus volvatus*. On Douglas-fir, *C. volvatus* is often associated with old bark beetle galleries and can be used as an indicator of bark beetle kill. Sporophores of *C. volvatus* could be confused with immature conks of other polypore fungi. The latter, however, are solid rather than "pouch-like." Insects have been shown to play a role in the dissemination of *C. volvatus* basidiospores.

References:

Borden, J. H. and M. McClaren. 1970. Biology of *Cryptoporus volvatus* (Peck.) Shear (Agaricales, Polyporaceae) in southwestern British Columbia: distribution, host species, and relationship with subcortical insects. Syesis 3: 145-154.

Gilbertson, R. L. and L. Ryvarden. 1986. North American Polypores. 1:220. Fungiflora, Oslo.

Figures 47a, 47b: Fruiting bodies of *Cryptoporus volvatus*, some dissected longitudinally to show the spore-producing surface "hidden" by a membrane. The pore through which spores are released is visible in 47b (arrow). Figure 47c: Fruiting bodies on the stem of a dead Douglas-fir.

Brown Cubical Sap Rot

Gleophyllum sepiarium (Wulfen:Fr.) P. Karst.

(= *Lenzites saepiaria* (Wulfen:Fr.) Fr.)

Basidiomycotina, Aphyllophorales, Polyporaceae

Hosts: *Gleophyllum sepiarium* is found primarily on dead conifer wood, less commonly on hardwoods. In B.C., it has been reported on amabilis, grand, and subalpine fir, white, black, Engelmann, and Sitka spruce, lodgepole, ponderosa, and western white pine, Douglas-fir, western redcedar, western hemlock, red alder, paper birch, aspen, and cherry. Elsewhere in North America it is also found on western larch, mountain hemlock, cypress, incense and yellow cedar, juniper, giant sequoia, apple, arbutus, elm, oak, sweet-gum, tulip-tree, and willow.

Distribution: This fungus is widely distributed on dead trees and slash throughout the range of its hosts in B.C.

Identification: The fruiting bodies are small, annual, leathery, shelf-like structures that generally form in cracks and checks on fallen logs (Figs. 48a, 48b). Occasionally, fruiting bodies are stalked. The upper surface is light-to-dark cinnamon brown, zoned, at first velvety but becoming roughened with maturity. The lower surface is light brown and consists of tough, radiating lamellae or gill-like structures (15-20/cm, counted at margin) (Fig. 48c). The context is brown.

The decay appears first as yellow to yellow-brown pockets of discoloration in the sapwood or outer heartwood. The advanced decay is a typical brown cubical rot, with yellow to yellow-brown mycelial felts in the shrinkage cracks.

Microscopic Characteristics: Hyphae in the context of the fruiting body are of three types: generative hyphae thin to thick-walled with clamps, skeletal hyphae (most common) thick-walled, up to 6.0 µm in diameter, binding hyphae golden-coloured, tortuous, rare. Basidiospores cylindrical, hyaline, smooth, IKI-, 9-13 × 3-5 µm. Growth in culture slow, mat at first white then yellow-brown, laccase negative, clamps, frequent arthroconidia. Stalpers: (2) (4) (7) (8) (9) (11) 13 (14) (15) (17) 18 (21) 22 24 (25) (26) 30 31 34 35 (37) (38) (39) 40 42 (44) (45) (46) 48 50 (51) 52 53 (54) (61) 67 (75) 83 84 85 (89) (90) (93) (95) (96) 98 100.

Damage: Extensive decay is indicated by the presence of fruiting bodies. Where conks are numerous, the entire sapwood and some heartwood should be considered unusable for lumber or pulp. Decay may also occur on wood in service, for example fence posts or other wooden structures.

Remarks: This fungus is occasionally found on living trees, and on dead sapwood under scars, but most commonly on fire-killed trees and slash. The fruiting bodies of *G. sepiarium* could be confused with *T. abietinum*, but the latter has fewer (8-13/cm) and coarser gills. Other related species of *Gloeophyllum* have a more pore-like hymenial surface rather than gills.

References:

Gilbertson, R. L. and L. Ryvarden. 1986. North American Polypores. 1:310. Fungiflora, Oslo.

Figures 48a, 48b: Fruiting bodies of *Gleophyllum sepiarium*.
Figure 48c: The spore-producing surface of *G. sepiarium* forms radiating lamellae.

Pitted Sap Rot

Trichaptum abietinum (Dickson:Fr.) Ryvarden

(= *Hirschioporus abietinus* (Dickson:Fr.) Donk)
(= *Polyporus abietinus* (Dickson:Fr.) Donk)

Basidiomycotina, Aphyllophorales, Polyporaceae

Hosts: Pitted sap rot is found in a wide range of coniferous hosts. In B.C., it has been reported on amabilis, grand and subalpine fir, western larch, white, black, and Sitka spruce, lodgepole, ponderosa, Scots, white-barked, and western white pine, Douglas-fir, western redcedar, western hemlock, *Arbutus*, and cherry. Elsewhere in North America it has also been found on mountain hemlock, California incense cedar, *Chamaecyparis thyoides*, beech, juniper, *Sequoia*, Engelmann spruce, and *Taxodium*.

Distribution: This fungus affects trees in all regions of the province.

Identification: Fruiting bodies rarely form on living trees but may be produced in great abundance on dead trees and forest litter. They are small (1-3 cm across), annual, thin, effused-reflexed, or shelf-like, forming abundantly in bark crevices. The upper surface is zoned, light grey and somewhat hairy in texture. On older specimens the upper surface may appear green from algal growth, or black (Fig. 49a). The lower surface is purple when fresh turning light brown with age. Pores are angular, 4-6 per mm, and with maturity the tissue between the pores tends to become elongated and torn into irregular spines or ridges (Figs. 49b, 49c).

In the early stage of decay, the wood becomes light-yellow to tan and soft. In the advanced stage, small pits develop, elongated in the direction of the grain, which may at first be filled with white fibrous material but later become empty. The cross section of the decay has a honeycomb appearance.

Microscopic Characteristics: Skeletal hyphae in the context of the fruiting body thick-walled, nonseptate, contextual generative hyphae thin-walled with clamps. Basidiospores cylindric, slightly curved, hyaline, smooth, IKI-, 6-7.5 × 2.5-3 µm. Growth in culture moderately rapid, mat white, translucent, laccase positive, clamps. Stalpers: 1 3 (7) (8) (11) 13 14 17 (18) 19 (21) 22 30 39 42 44 (45) (46) 48 52 53 54 57 72 (81) 82 83 (89) 90 (94).

Damage: The fungus is of primary importance as a deteriorating agent but is also capable of causing sap rot and heart rot in living trees. Extensive decay of sapwood is indicated by the presence of fruiting bodies. It has been reported to have caused decay in unseasoned wood in service.

Remarks: The decay caused by this fungus is restricted to the sapwood; fruiting bodies often form a complete ring on the sapwood of the cut ends of logs. The fruiting bodies of *T. abietinum* could be confused with those of *Stereum sanguinolentum*. The hymenium of the latter will turn red when bruised. Earlier taxonomic treatments of *T. abietinum* were broad, and included fungi now recognized as separate species (*T. fuscoviolaceum* and *T. laricinum*). Many reports of *T. abietinum* may be these species.

References:
Gilbertson, R. L. and L. Ryvarden. 1987. North American Polypores. 2:768. Fungiflora, Oslo.

Figure 49a: Old fruiting bodies of *Trichaptum abietinum* with algae growing on the upper surface.
Figure 49b: A mass of fruiting bodies in typical abundance on a dead Douglas-fir stem.
Figure 49c: The ridged pore layer of *T. abietinum* fruiting bodies.

Cedar Leaf Blight

Didymascella thujina (E. J. Durand) Maire

(= *Keithia thujina* E. J. Durand)

Ascomycotina, Rhytismatales, Hypodermataceae

Hosts: *Didymascella thujina* is found only on western redcedar in B.C. Elsewhere in North America it is also reported on northern white-cedar and Oriental Arborvitae.

Distribution: This fungus is widely distributed throughout the range of western redcedar in B.C.

Identification: The disease appears on trees of all sizes, but most commonly on young seedlings and the lower branches of older trees. Symptoms first appear in the spring on 1-year old foliage as bleached, tan-brown areas on individual scale-leaves. The infected brown leaves are usually conspicuous against the healthy green foliage (Fig. 50a). Fruiting bodies (apothecia) become readily visible by June as olive-brown (maturing to black) spots on the upper surface of infected leaves (Fig. 50b). Usually one, but up to three apothecia form on each leaf. Twigs with heavily infected leaves are generally shed in the autumn. On diseased leaves that remain, apothecia often shrivel and drop out, leaving dark pits.

Microscopic Characteristics: Ascomata mainly on upper surface of needles, subepidermal, roughly circular in outline, olive-brown, up to 1 mm in diameter; hymenium not covered by fungal tissue, exposed by rupture of overlying epidermis. Ascomata may fall out completely when spent leaving a pit in the leaf. Asci clavate, 2-spored, pore not blue in iodine (J-), 100 × 20 μm. Ascospores ellipsoid, thick-walled, 1-septate near the upper end, walls pitted, brown, 22-25 × 15-16 μm, with a gelatinous sheath. Paraphyses filiform, branched, thickened at the tips.

Damage: Young seedlings and saplings sustain the most damage where stem or branch death may occur. Disease on trees older than 4-5 years can retard growth. Disease levels are highest in dense stands where humidity levels are high. Such conditions can occur in forest nurseries where the disease can be a serious problem.

Remarks: Cedar leaf blight (also known as Keithia blight) can be confused with normal foliage colour changes that occur on western redcedar in the autumn. However, seasonal colour changes affect the entire plant in contrast to the scattered symptoms of the disease.

References:

Kope, H. H. and J. R. Sutherland. 1994. Keithia blight; review of the disease, and research on container grown western redcedar in British Columbia, Canada. *In* Diseases and Insects in Forest Nurseries. R. Perrin and J. R. Sutherland, eds. INRA Editions, Paris. pp. 27-44.

Figure 50a: Western redcedar infected with *Didymascella thujina*. Figure 50b: Apothecia of *D. thujina* on western redcedar scale-leaves.

Elytroderma Needle Cast

Elytroderma deformans (Weir) Darker

(= *Hypoderma deformans* Weir)

Ascomycotina, Rhytismatales, Hypodermataceae

Hosts: This disease is restricted to "hard" or "two- and three-needle" pine species. In B.C., *Elytroderma deformans* has been reported on **lodgepole** and **ponderosa pine**. Elsewhere in North America it has also been found on big-cone, jack, Jeffrey, knobcone, Mexican stone, pinyon, and short-leaf pine.

Distribution: Most collections of this disease are from the central interior and Kootenays. Minor damage is reported for the coast and Yukon; little or none from the north central interior.

Identification: Infection takes place in the late summer but symptoms do not appear until early spring of the following year. Groups of needles turn red and die, forming conspicuous flags (Figs. 51a, 51b). The fungus is perennial in the twigs, often stimulating them to form relatively small, open and tufted witches brooms (Figs. 51c, 51d). Fruiting bodies develop as small dark streaks on the dead foliage (Fig. 51e).

Microscopic Characteristics: Ascomata appear as narrow, black lines of varying lengths, chiefly on the abaxial surface of the browned needles, up to 10 mm long; opening by a longitudinal slit to expose the pale brown hymenium. The subepidermal clypeus of black cells covers only the central part of the hymenium. The subhymenium is hyaline and thin. Asci saccate to fusiform-clavate, 8-spored, 140-240 × 30-45 µm. Ascospores hyaline, cylindric, 1-septate, 90-120 × 6-9 µm, with thick gelatinous sheath. Paraphyses filiform, simple, septate. Conidiomata concolorous with needle, subepidermal, up to 1.2 mm long, blister-like. Conidiophores 12-15 µm long, arising from a thin basal layer, ampuliform, simple. Conidia terminal, hyaline, bacillar, 6-8 × 1 µm.

Damage: Damage is caused by branch and stem deformation, and growth reduction resulting from defoliation. Although the impact of the disease is highest on young trees or trees with poor crowns, infected mature trees may be predisposed to root disease or bark beetle attack. Diseased trees are also considered to have negative visual impact in high-value recreation sites.

Remarks: The incidence of this disease is highest where moist environmental conditions prevail, often near lakes and streams.

References:

Hunt, R. S. 1978. Elytroderma disease of pines. Can. For. Serv., Forest Pest Leaf. No. 27. Victoria, B.C.

Figures 51a, 51b: Discoloured needles resulting from infection by *Elytroderma deformans*.

Figures 51c, 51d: Broom symptoms of Elytroderma needle cast.

Figure 51e: Slit-like fruiting bodies of *E. deformans*.

Brown Felt Blight

Herpotrichia juniperi (Duby) Petr.
(= *Herpotrichia nigra* R. Hartig)
Neopeckia coulteri (Peck) Sacc. in Peck
(= *Herpotrichia coulteri* (Peck) Bose)

Ascomycotina, Dothideales, Pleosporaceae

Hosts: *Herpotrichia juniperi* is found only on conifers. In B.C., it has been reported on amabilis and subalpine fir, yellow cedar, juniper, Engelmann, Sitka, and white spruce, lodgepole pine, yew, and mountain and western hemlock. Elsewhere in North America it has also been reported on grand fir, incense-cedar, mountain heather, Douglas-fir, western white pine,and western red-cedar. *Neopeckia coulteri* is generally found only on pines. In B.C., on lodgepole and white-bark pine. Elsewhere in North America, on Engelmann spruce and western white pine.

Distribution: These fungi are widely distributed throughout the range of their hosts in B.C., particularly at higher altitudes.

Identification: These diseases are readily identified by the brown, felt-like masses of mycelium that cover twigs and branches (Figs. 52a, 52b). Fungal growth is prolific on branches that are buried under snow. As the snow melts, and felts are exposed, fungal development ceases. Under the snow, the mycelium is grey in colour. Freshly exposed felts are dark brown-black, weathering to grey-brown. Spherical black fruiting bodies develop on and in mycelial mats the second year after formation, but are very difficult to see. The macroscopic signs and symptoms of both diseases are very similar; the two are differentiated by host preference and microscopic features.

Microscopic Characteristics: *Herpotrichia juniperi*: Pseudothecia dark brown, globose, partially hidden in a felt-like subiculum of dark brown hyphae, 200-450 μm diameter, with a definite apical pore, wall of polygonal cells 20-40 μm thick, covered with brown, septate hyphae. Asci cylindrical to subclavate, 8-spored, bitunicate, 115-190 × 12-18 μm. Ascospores uniseriate or obliquely biseriate, hyaline and 1-septate at first, becoming brown and 3-4 septate, elliptical, constricted at median septum, with a mucous sheath, 25-34 × 8-12 μm. Pseudoparaphyses filiform, hyaline.

Neopeckia coulteri: Pseudothecia dark brown, globose, single or in small groups, formed on a subiculum of felty brown hyphae, 250-500 μm diameter, with a distinctly papillate pore, wall of thick-walled pseudoparenchyma, covered by brown hyphae. Asci cylindrical, short-stalked, 8-spored, bitunicate, 140-210 × 14-20 μm. Ascospores monostichous, elliptical, dark brown, 1-septate, constricted, with a dark epispore, 10-28 × 7-10 μm. Pseudoparaphyses hyaline, filiform, sparsely branched.

Damage: Branch dieback or death occurs on seedlings and the lower branches of larger trees. Although rarely a problem in natural forests, this disease can cause significant loss in bareroot nurseries and young plantations where sufficient snow is present.

Remarks: Another "snow mould" that occurs on true firs and Douglas-fir is *Phacidium abietis* (Dearn.) Reid & Cain, but it does not invade branches or cause dieback.

References:
Sims, H. R. 1967. On the ecology of *Herpotrichia nigra*. Mycologia 59:902-909.

Figure 52a, 52b: Brown felt-like mycelial masses characteristic of *Herpotrichia juniperi* covering needles and branches of spruce (Fig. 52a) and subalpine fir (Fig. 52b).

Pine Needle Cast

Lophodermella concolor (Dearn.) Darker
(= *Hypodermella concolor* (Dearn.) Darker)

Ascomycotina, Rhytismatales, Hypodermataceae

Hosts: *Lophodermella concolor* is restricted to hard or two-needle pine species. In B.C., pine needle cast has been reported on **lodgepole**, **ponderosa**, and **Scots** pine.

Distribution: This disease is common in all regions of the province, particularly in the southern interior.

Identification: Infected stands have reddish discoloured foliage in May and June, turning straw-coloured by July (Figs. 53a, 53b). As the summer progresses, diseased needles on previous years growth are shed while new growth remains giving branches a "lion's tail" appearance (Fig. 53c).

Although new needles are infected during their first year of growth, there is little visual evidence of infection at this time. Damage occurs in the needle tissue over the winter, and needles turn red in the spring. Fruiting bodies (apothecia) are formed on dead and dying needles, appearing as shallow oval depressions that are concolorous with the needle surface (hence the name *concolor*) (Fig. 53d). Infected needles are shed at about the time that the apothecia mature, and spores are released during periods of wet weather, infecting new growth.

Microscopic Characteristics: Apothecia (hysterothecia) subhypodermal, concolorous, 0.4-0.8 × 0.3-0.4 mm, opening by a single slit. Asci subcylindric, 120-225 × 15-17 μm; ascospores unicellular, clavate, colourless, 45-60 × 4-8 μm.

Damage: Significant levels of defoliation occur in years following periods of moist summer weather favorable for infection. Increment loss and mortality may occur after repeated epidemics, particularly in young trees.

Remarks: Other fungi, including *Hemiphacidium longisporum* Ziller and Funk and *Hendersonia pinicola* Wehm., often invade needles infected with *L. concolor,* competing with, or parasitizing the *Lophodermium* (Fig. 53e). A related species of *Lophodermella*, *L. montivaga* Petre., can be distinguished from *L. concolor* by its elongate, brown fruiting structures, and that it tends to have a more northern distribution in the province.

References:

Hunt, R. S. 1995. Pine needle casts and blights in the Pacific region. Can. For. Serv., Forest Pest Leaf. No. 43. Victoria, B.C.

Figures 53a, 53b: Lodgepole pine infected with *Lophodermella concolor.* Figure 53c: "Lion's tail" appearance of branches after infected needles are shed. Figure 53d: Concolorous fruiting bodies of *L. concolor.* Figure 53e: Lodgepole pine needles infected with both *L. concolor* and *Hendersonia pinicola* (black spots).

Dothistroma Needle Blight

Mycosphaerella pini Rost. in Munk

(= *Scirrhia pini* Funk & Parker)

(Anamorph = *Dothistroma septospora* (Dorog.) Morelet)

Ascomycotina, Dothidiales, Dothidiaceae

Hosts: *Mycosphaerella pini* is found only on pines. In B.C., it has been reported on lodgepole, Jeffrey, ponderosa, Monterey, black, bishop, and maritime pine as well as some hybrid pine species. Elsewhere in North America it has also been found on shortleaf, red, western white, and Scots pine and in rare cases on Douglas-fir, European larch, and Sitka spruce.

Distribution: This fungus is widely distributed throughout the range of its hosts in B.C.

Identification: Trees affected by Dothistroma needle blight tend to have thin crowns with dis-coloured and dead needles (Fig. 54a). The lower crown is often the most severely affected (Fig. 54b). Infection of needles of all ages occurs throughout the year at the coast and from spring to autumn in the interior, resulting in the development of yellow-brown to red-brown lesions or bands (Fig. 54c). The red colour is due to the presence of a fungal toxin. A character-istic feature of the lesions is the abrupt change from diseased to healthy green needle tissue. Needle tips distal to lesions die and turn brown, while the base of the needles generally remain green (Fig. 54d). Fruiting bodies (stromata) form on dead needles appearing as small black structures breaking through the epidermis. Older diseased needles are shed, often forming "lion's-tail" branches, with only terminal needles remaining.

Microscopic Characteristics: Ascostromata black, multiloculate, subepidermal, erumpent, 200-600 × 95-150 μm; tissues pseudoparenchymatous, cells 7-14 μm diameter; locules globose, in longitudinal order, 40-86 μm diameter. Asci cylindric or clavate, bitunicate, apex rounded, 8-spored, 46-52 × 8-10 μm. Ascospores hyaline, 1-septate, fusiform to cuneate, 13-16 × 3-4 μm. Conidial stromata linear, subepidermal, erumpent, dark brown or black, 125-1500 μm long, 5-45 μm wide, up to 600 μm high. Conidial locules parallel to the longitudinal axis of stroma, without a distinct wall. Conidia hyaline, 1- to 5- but usually 3-septate, blunt at the ends, straight, slightly curved or bent, 16-64 × 3.5 μm. Conidiophores numerous, approximate-ly the same size as the conidia, hyaline or amber, dense, unbranched, producing conidia at their tips.

Damage: Where environmental conditions favour infection, this disease can spread rapidly and cause significant damage. Trees can be defoliated within weeks, and mortality is common with repeated attacks.

Remarks: This disease is also commonly known as red band needle blight. The life-cycle is com-pleted in 1 year at the coast but requires 2 years in most other parts of the continent. The fun-gus causing the disease is most commonly observed in its conidial state (*Dothistroma septospora*).

References:

Funk, A. 1985. Foliar fungi of western trees. Can. For. Serv., Inf. Rep. BC-X-265.

Figure 54a: Lodgepole pine plantation affected by *Mycosphaerella pini* in east-central B.C.
Figure 54b: Lower crown discoloration typical of *Mycosphaerella*-infected western white pine.
Figure 54c: Red banding symptoms on infected needles. Figure 54d: *Mycosphaerella*-infected needles with discoloured tips and green needle bases. Figure 54e: Fruiting bodies of *M. pini* on western white pine needles.

Douglas-fir Needle Blight

Rhabdocline pseudotsugae Syd.

Ascomycotina, Rhytismatales, Hypodermataceae

Hosts: Douglas-fir needle blight occurs on both coastal and interior forms of Douglas-fir but is less severe on the coastal form.

Distribution: This fungus is widely distributed throughout the range of Douglas-fir in B.C.

Identification: Severely attacked trees usually have chlorotic foliage and very thin and open crowns (Figs. 55a, 55b). Infection takes place in the new foliage in the spring. Chlorotic, yellow spots 1-2 mm in diameter appear on both surfaces of 1st year needles in the fall, coalescing and darkening to red-brown during the winter (Fig. 55c). Some needles are shed during the winter. On needles that are retained, fruiting bodies (apothecia) form in the late spring. Apothecia are small, orange-brown, raised pustules, generally occurring on the lower side but occasionally on the upper side of needles (Fig. 55d). Spores are released in May or June, after which infected needles are shed. Identification is easiest in the late spring when needle spots and apothecia are visible.

Microscopic Characteristics: Apothecia chiefly hypophyllous, orange to red-brown, on one or both sides of needle midrib; erumpent by median splitting of overlying epidermis, or by circumsissile or lateral splitting when apothecia small; hypothecium poorly developed, no epithecial tissue, excipulum of marginal paraphyses only; situated in necrotic spots that are roughly circular, band-like or extending up to the entire length of needle, discrete or confluent in the necrotic spots, 0.5-10 long × 0.3-0.6 wide mm. Asci clavate, broadest below apex which is flattened, 8-spored, opening by a psuedooperculum or a bilabiate split of the apex, does not stain with iodine (J-), 120-160 × 16-22 µm. Ascospores at first hyaline and 1-celled, becoming 2-celled with one cell turning dark brown, oblong with obtuse ends, slightly constricted at the middle, 13-19 × 5-8 µm with a thick gelatinous sheath. Paraphyses septate, up to 2.5 µm thick, sometimes swollen at the tips, extending beyond the asci to form an epithecium.

Damage: Repeated severe infection almost completely defoliates trees, leaving only the current years needles. The impact of the disease therefore, is greatest on small trees because of their smaller total number of needles; large trees usually undergo only light defoliation and sustain little damage. Christmas tree plantations can be severely damaged.

Remarks: Douglas-fir needle blight is caused by a number of species and subspecies of the genus *Rhabdocline*. The most common in B.C. is *R. pseudotsugae* described here, and *R. weirii* (Parker & Reid). The symptoms caused by these organisms are similar, however, so precise identification is seldom important. Epidemic infection years occur in cycles and depend on climatic conditions during the infection period. Occasionally individual trees show marked resistance to the disease.

References:
Collis, D. G. 1971. Rhabdocline needle cast of Douglas-fir in British Columbia. Can. For. Serv., Forest Pest Leaf. No. 32. Victoria, B.C.

Parker, A. K. and J. Reid. 1969. The genus *Rhabdocline* Syd. Can. J. Bot. 47: 1533-1545.

Figure 55a: Thin crowns on Douglas-fir infected by *Rhabdocline pseudotsugae*. Figure 55b: Defoliation caused by *R. pseudotsugae*. Figure 55c: Red-brown spots on *Rhabdocline*-infected Douglas-fir needles. Figure 55d: *R. pseudotsugae* fruiting bodies.

Larch Needle Diseases

Meria laricis Vuill. (Larch needle cast)

Deuteromycotina, Hyphomycetes, Tuberculariales

Hypodermella laricis Tub. (Larch needle blight)

Ascomycotina, Rhytismatales, Hypodermataceae

Hosts: *Meria laricis* is found almost exclusively on western larch, and rarely on alpine larch *Hypodermella laricis* has been reported on western larch in B.C. and on alpine larch and tamarack elsewhere in North America.

Distribution: These fungi are found throughout the range of larch in B.C.; mainly the southern interior with some collections at the coast.

Identification: Needles affected by both of these diseases suddenly turn yellow and then red-brown in the spring and early summer (Figs. 56a, 56b). *Meria laricis:* Infected needles are generally shed soon after they turn brown. Clusters of spores (conidia) may be visible with a hand lens on the lower surface of needles, as white dots associated with stomata. These can be distinguished from stomatal structures by staining with cotton blue. Fallen needles should be examined as they are an important source of inoculum.

Hypodermella laricis: Fruiting bodies (hysterothecia) form soon after needles are killed and turn brown, appearing as elliptical black spots (Fig. 56c). In contrast with *Meria laricis*, diseased needles are retained after normal needle drop in the fall (Fig. 56d).

Microscopic Characteristics: *Meria laricis:* Conidiophores originating from substomatal mycelial masses and emerging from the stomates in dense tufts, simple or dichotomously branched, hyaline, septate, frequently curved, up to 45 µm long, 2-3 µm wide. Conidiogenous cells monophialidic, apical or intercalary, indeterminate, + cylindrical, apertures typically produced immediately below the septa on a short sterigma. Conidia hyaline, cylindrical with a median constriction (hence, peanut- or dumb-bell-shaped), non-septate but becoming 1-septate at germination, 9-13 × 3-4 µm.

Hypodermella laricis: Hysterothecia black, elliptical, subcuticular, more or less in a continuous row, 0.5-0.8 × 0.2-0.3 µm; a basal layer of brown pseudoparenchyma subtends a plectenchymatous layer 10-15 µm thick below the hymenium; covering layer dark without an evident opening mechanism. Asci clavate, usually 4-spored, acutely pointed at maturity, 80-112 × 20-24 µm. Ascospores clavate tapering to an acute base, hyaline, nonseptate, with a gelatinous sheath 5 µm thick, 70-105 × 6 µm. Paraphyses shorter than the asci, filiform, slightly swollen at the tips. Pycnidia black, numerous, 120-300 × 80-120 µm. Conidia hyaline, elongated pyriform, 4-5 × 1 µm.

Damage: Neither of these diseases kill large trees, but repeated infections can result in growth reduction. Significant mortality of nursery seedlings has been caused by *Meria laricis.*

Remarks: Both diseases may be present on the same needles. The rapid onset of disease symptoms could be confused with frost damage. Frost damage, however, tends to kill both needles and young stems, and no fruiting bodies are formed. Several rust fungi including *Melampsora occidentalis, M. albertensis*, and *M. paradoxa* Diet. & Holw. are also found on larch. These can be distinguished by their spore-producing fruiting structures (aecia).

References:

Garbutt, R. W. 1995. Foliage diseases in western larch in British Columbia. Can. For. Serv., Forest Pest Leaf. No. 71. Victoria, B.C.

Figure 56a: Discoloured foliage of western larch affected by *Hypodermella laricis*. Figure 56b: Needle discoloration and defoliation of western larch infected by *Meria laricis*. Figure 56c: Hysterothecia of *H. laricis* on dead western larch needles. Figure 56d: Dead needles infected by *H. laricis* retained on western larch.

Other Needle Casts and Blights

A number of other fungal diseases affecting conifer needles are common throughout B.C. Although generally less damaging than the diseases described in the previous pages, localized epidemics can result in significant economic loss.

Fungal Organism	B.C. Hosts	Identification
Lophodermium pinastri (Shrad.:Fr.) Chev.	all pines	Oval, black fruiting bodies scattered over dead needles, separated by shiny black, transverse lines (Fig. 57a).
Lophodermium seditiosum Minter, Staley, & Millar	black, maritime and red pine	Similar to *L. pinastri*, but transverse lines are lacking or brownish.
Davisomycella ampla (J. J. Davis) Darke	lodgepole pine	Oval, black fruiting bodies form on straw-coloured portions of needles. These areas are often separated from green tissue by an orange-brown band (Fig. 57b).
Bifusella linearis (Peck) Höhn.	whitebark and western white pine	Long, black, shiny fruiting bodies form on needles
Lirula macrospora (R. Hartig) Darker	white, black, Sitka, and Engelmann spruce	Fruiting bodies appear as elongate black lines, often running the full length of needles which remain on the twigs after they have been killed (Fig. 57c).
Delphinella abietis (Rostr.) E. Müller *Delphinella balsameae* (Waterm.) E. Müller	subalpine fir	Young fir shoots are killed soon after they appear, but spores are not produced on the needles until the following spring (Fig. 57d).

References:

Funk, A. 1985. Foliar fungi of western trees. Can. For. Serv., Inf. Rep. BC-X-265.

Hunt, R. S. 1995. Common pine needle casts and blights in the Pacific region. Can. For. Serv., Forest Pest Leaf. No. 43. Victoria, B.C.

Ziller, W. G. and R. S. Hunt. 1977. Lophodermium needle cast of pines in nurseries and plantations. Can. For. Serv., Forest Pest Leaf. No. 52. Victoria, B.C.

Figure 57a: *Lophodermium sp.* on lodgepole pine. Figure 57b: Fruiting bodies of *Davisomycella ampla* on lodgepole pine. Figure 57c: Fruiting bodies of *Lirula macrospora* on Sitka spruce.
Figure 57d: Symptoms of Delphinella blight on subalpine fir.

Conifer - Aspen Rust

Melampsora albertensis Arth.

Basidiomycotina, Uredinales, Melampsoraceae

Hosts: In B.C., the principal aecial hosts of *Melampsora albertensis* are Douglas-fir and larch, but the rust has also been shown to infect species of pine, fir, spruce, and hemlock (in order of decreasing susceptibility). Inoculation studies by Ziller (1965) demonstrated the broad conifer host range of this rust. The telial host in B.C. is trembling aspen, and in other parts of North America, eastern cottonwood.

Distribution: This fungus is widely distributed throughout B.C. where both telial and aecial hosts are present.

Identification: Conifer hosts are infected shortly after bud-break, and spermogonia and aecia appear within 2 weeks on slightly chlorotic needles (Figs. 58a, 58b). Needles become increasingly discoloured and shriveled as aeciospores mature, and soon die and are shed during the summer. Uredinia begin to appear on aspen leaves soon after aeciospore release, forming yellow leaf spots (Fig. 58c). Urediniospores reinfect aspen throughout the summer and when the rust is severe, entire leaf surfaces become yellow (Fig. 58d). In late summer, brown-coloured telia form in the place of uredinia. Necrosis of surrounding leaf tissue often accompanies the formation of telia.

Microscopic Characteristics: Spermogonia subcuticular, on all surfaces of current years needles, inconspicuous. Aecia mainly on lower surfaces of needles, round or oblong, yellow. Aeciospores with orange-yellow contents, globoid, minutely verrucose, 16-21 × 19-26 μm. Uredinia mainly on lower surfaces of leaves, orange-yellow when fresh. Urediniospores with orange-yellow contents, ellipsoid or ovoid, laterally flattened, with both smooth and verrucose sides, 15-23 × 23-35 μm. Telia on lower leaf surfaces, teliospores cinnamon-brown, smooth, 10-15 × 29-45 μm.

Damage: *Melampsora albertensis* can cause considerable damage to conifer hosts, particularly in nursery settings. Disease levels can be reduced if infected aspen is removed from the vicinity. Recently *M. medusae* f. sp. *deltoides* was reported on cottonwood and many hybrid poplar clones in commercial plantations in Oregon, Washington, and B.C. The presence of this pathogenic form of the rust presents a serious threat to hybrid poplar plantations and may necessitate the replacement of susceptible clones.

Remarks: There is some question as to whether *M. medusae* Thuem and *M. albertensis* are the same species. Because of the similarities in life-cycle and host preference, they are considered together in this book. Another poplar leaf rust, *Melampsora occidentalis,* infects similar conifer hosts but differs from *M. albertensis* in aeciospore size and telial hosts. *Melampsora albertensis* aeciospores are shorter and they infect only aspen.

References:
Ziller, W. G. 1974. The tree rusts of western Canada. Can. For. Serv., Publ. No. 1329. Victoria, B.C.

Figure 58a: Discoloured foliage on Douglas-fir infected with *Melampsora albertensis*. Figure 58b: *M. albertensis* aecia on lodgepole pine neeedles. Figures 58c, 58d: Uredinia on aspen leaves.

Willow–Conifer Rust

Melampsora epitea Thuem.

Basidiomycotina, Uredinales, Melampsoraceae

Hosts: In B.C. and throughout North America, the aecial hosts of *Melampsora epitea* include mountain and western hemlock, amabilis, balsam, white, grand, and subalpine fir, tamarack, alpine and western larch. The telial hosts include many species of willow.

Distribution: This fungus is widely distributed throughout the range of its hosts in B.C.

Identification: Spermagonia and aecia appear on conifer hosts on new needles shortly after bud-break. Aecia are yellow-orange and differ from other conifer-needle rusts in that the whitish blister or tube-like covering (peridium) is rudimentary or lacking. Uredinia are readily observed throughout the summer on the underside of willow leaves as yellow-orange pustules (Figs. 59a, 59b). Since uredinial mycelium can overwinter on willow leaves, urediniospores produced in the spring can continue to infect willows from year-to-year; the rust does not need to alternate to the conifer host.

Microscopic Characteristics: Spermagonia and aecia on current years needles, occasionally on cones. Spermagonia originating under the epidermis. Aeciospores 14-21 × 15-24 µm; wall thickened at the apex. Uredinia and telia hypophyllous. Urediniospores globoid to broadly ellipsoid, 12-17 × 14-20 µm; wall uniformly thick. Teliospores 6-14 × 16-30 µm, wall uniformly thick.

Damage: Damage to conifer hosts is minimal, infections are usually sparse and restricted to regeneration and the lower branches of saplings. Although the severity of the disease on willow is undocumented, it is likely that damage to willow plantations could be as high as that caused by *M. albertensis* on poplars.

Remarks: Willow rusts are often treated as one species complex, loosely called *Melampsora epitea*, since their uredinial and telial states on willow are indistinguishable. When aecial hosts are determined through inoculation tests, several species may be delimited from this complex. Using this approach, the following species are recognized:

Rust name	Aecial Host
Melampsora abieti-capraearum	true firs
Melampsora epitea f. sp. *tsugae*	western and mountain hemlock
Melampsora paradoxa	Tamarack, alpine, and western larch
Melampsora ribesii-purpureae	currant and gooseberry

Melampsora abieti-capraearum frequently appears together with *Pucciniastrum epilobii* on fir. The willow rust on conifers can be distinguished by naked aecia (lacking peridia.. At the microscopic level, willow rusts can be distinguished from other Melampsora rusts on conifers. The other rusts exhibit bilateral thickening of the aeciospore walls, whereas willow rusts have no bilateral thickening.

References:
Ziller, W. G. 1974. The tree rusts of western Canada. Can. For. Serv., Publ. No. 1329. Victoria, B.C.

Figures 59a, 59b: Uredinia of *Melampsora epitea* on willow leaves.

Conifer - Cottonwood Rust

Melampsora occidentalis Jacks.

Basidiomycotina, Uredinales, Melampsoraceae

Hosts: In B.C., the principal aecial hosts of *Melampsora occidentalis* are European, Japanese, and western larch, Douglas-fir, Sitka spruce, lodgepole, sugar, western white, ponderosa, and Monterey pine (in order of decreasing susceptibility). The telial hosts in B.C. are black cottonwood, balsam poplar, and some hybrid poplars. Telial hosts in other parts of North America include Fremont and lanceleaf cottonwoods, as well as Carolina poplar species.

Distribution: This fungus is widely distributed throughout the range of its hosts in B.C.

Identification: Conifer hosts are infected shortly after bud-break, and spermogonia and aecia appear within 2 weeks on slightly chlorotic needles (Fig. 60a). Needles become increasingly discoloured and shriveled as aeciospores mature, and soon die and are shed during the summer (Fig. 60b). Uredinia begin to appear on poplar leaves soon after aeciospore release, forming yellow leaf spots. (Figs. 60c, 60d) Urediniospores reinfect poplar throughout the summer and when the rust is severe, entire leaf surfaces become yellow. In late summer, brown-coloured telia form in the place of uredinia. Necrosis of surrounding leaf tissue often accompanies the formation of telia. In the spring, teliospores germinate to produce basidia and basidiospores, which infect conifer hosts.

Microscopic Characteristics: Spermagonia subcuticular, on current years needles. Aecia hypophyllous, round or ellipsoid, orange-yellow. Aeciospores with orange-yellow contents, broadly ellipsoid, slightly flattened laterally, 22-27 × 26-35 µm, walls hyaline, verrucose, 1.5-2.5 µm thick, flattened side walls 3-6 µm thick. Uredinia hypophyllous, round, orange-yellow when fresh. Urediniospores with orange-yellow contents, ellipsoid, oblong, or pyriform, 16-29 × 32-48 µm, wall laterally flattened, wall colourless, echinulate with or without smooth spots. Telia hypophyllous, small, round, waxy, cinnamon-brown. Teliospores prismatic, 10-20 × 40-64 µm, wall cinnamon-brown, 1-2 µm thick at sides, 3-5 µm thick and darker at apex.

Damage: *Melampsora occidentalis*, like the other Melampsora rusts, causes more serious damage to hardwoods than to its conifer hosts.

Remarks: The aecia and telia of *Melampsora occidentalis* are macroscopically similar to those of *M. albertensis and M. medusa*. However, the aeciospores and urediniospores of *M. occidentalis* are significantly larger.

References:

Ziller, W. G. 1955. Studies of western tree rusts II. *Melampsora occidentalis* and *M. albertensis*, two needle rusts of Douglas-fir. Can J. Bot. 33:177-188.

Ziller, W. G. 1974. The tree rusts of western Canada. Can. For. Serv., Publ. No. 1329. Victoria, B.C.

Figure 60a: Aecia and spermogonia of *Melampsora occidentalis* on Monterey pine seedling.
Figure 60b: Douglas-fir heavily infected by *M. occidentalis*. Figure 60c: Yellow discoloration of leaves associated with uredinia on cottonwood. Figure 60d: *Melampsora occidentalis* uredinia on cottonwood leaves.

Aspen and Poplar Leaf and Twig Blight

Venturia macularis (Fr.) E. Müller & Arx
(= *Venturia tremulae* Aderh.)
(anamorph = *Pollaccia radiosa* (Lib.) Bald & Cif.)
Venturia populina (Vuill.) Fabric.
(anamorph = *Pollaccia elegans* Servazzi)

Ascomycotina, Dothideales, Venturiaceae

Hosts: In B.C., *Venturia macularis* has been reported on aspen. Elsewhere in North America it has also been found on bigtooth aspen, white poplar, hybrid poplars, and eastern cottonwood. Throughout North America *Venturia populina* has been reported on balsam and lombardy poplar, cottonwood, and poplar hybrids.

Distribution: These fungi are widely distributed throughout the range of their hosts in B.C.

Identification: In the spring, young shoots and succulent terminal leaves wilt and turn black. Killed shoots droop, forming a characteristic shepherd's crook symptom (Figs. 61a, 61b, 61c). Lesions on shoots and leaves turn brownish black-olive green indicating the development of conidia. Perithecia with ascospores form on dead tissues in the fall and winter. Infections of *V. macularis* on aspen are primarily on terminal shoots on trees less than 3 m tall. *Venturia populina* infections occur on both terminal and lateral shoots throughout the crown of trees of all ages and sizes when environmental conditions favour infection (Fig. 61d).

Microscopic Characteristics: *Venturia macularis:* Ascomata immersed, globose to conical, erumpent, glabrous or setose, wall of brown polygonal cells, 80-140 µm diameter, setae 30-50 µm long, apical pore 25-50 µm wide. Asci oblong to saccate, bitunicate, 2-4-8-spored, 42-63 × 10-12 µm. Ascospores greenish-to-brown, elliptical to clavate, straight or inequilateral, 1-septate in the middle or below, slightly constricted, sometimes finely roughened, sometimes with a gelatinous coating, 8-14 × 4.5-6 µm. Acervuli irregular, olive-green. Conidiophores brown, non-septate, 8-12 × 4-6 µm. Conidia brown, ellipsoid to cylindrical, straight or bent, 0-2 septate, 12-22 × 6-7 µm.

Venturia populina: similar to *V. macularis* but with larger ascospores (20-23 × 11-13 µm) and straight conidia (25-36 × 8-14 µm).

Damage: When moist weather conditions prevail during the growing season, *V. macularis* can kill most shoots in aspen stands regenerating by sprouting. Repeated infection results in stem deformity and growth reduction. These diseases are most severe in young stands, and have the greatest impact in intensively managed plantations.

References:

Dance, B. W. 1961. Leaf and shoot blight of poplars (section *Tacamahaca*) caused by *Venturia populina* (Vuill.) Fabric. Can. J. Bot. 39:875-890.

Figures 61a, 61b, 61c: Necrotic shoots and leaves on aspen caused by *Venturia macularis*. Note characteristic "Shepherd's crook" symptoms. Figure 61d: Defoliation caused by *V. populina*.

Other Broadleaf Foliar Diseases

Several other fungal diseases affecting the foliage of broadleaf trees are common throughout B.C. In general these diseases cause little damage in natural forests, but localized epidemics can result in significant economic loss in stands of broadleaf trees under intensive management.

Fungal Organism	B.C. Hosts	Identification
Ciborinia whetzelii (Seaver) Seaver	aspen, cottonwood	Sclerotia form dark "inkspots" on living leaves that drop out in late summer leaving "shotholes" (Fig. 62a).
Didymosporium arbuticola Zeller	arbutus	Leaf spots, brown with purplish to reddish margins, 3-6 mm diameter form on living leaves (Fig. 62b).
Discula destructiva Redlin	dogwood	Tan-coloured spots and necrotic blotches form on leaves (Fig. 62c). Infections often progress to shoots and stems
Marssonina populi (Lib.) Magnus teliomorph = *Drepanopeziza populorum* (Demaz.) Höhn.	aspen, cottonwood, hybrid poplars	Diffuse orange-brown spots, 2-5 mm diameter, coalesce into vein-limited blotches (Fig. 62d).
Linospora tetraspora G. E. Thompson	cottonwood, balsam poplar	Irregular blotches of brownish grey discoloured tissue along leaf veins. Scattered black stromata appear as black dots, 0.1 mm diameter (Fig. 62e).

Table continued on page 134

Figure 62a: Sclerotia of *Ciborinia whetzelii* on aspen. Figure 62b: Leaf spots on arbutus caused by *Didymosporium arbuticola*. Figure 62c: Dogwood anthracnose caused by *Discula destructiva*.
Figure 62d: Leaf spot symptoms on hybrid poplar caused by *Marssonina populi*. Figure 62e: Stromata of *Linospora tetraspora* on discoloured leaf tissue.

Fungal Organism	B.C. Hosts	Identification
Mycosphaerella populicola G. E. Thompson anamorph = *Septoria populicola* Peck	balsam and hybrid poplars, rarely aspen	Circular black leaf spots form on both sides of leaves (Fig. 62f).
Rhytisma punctatum (Pers.:Fr.) Fr.	bigleaf maple	Stromata appear as "tar spots" on roughly circular areas of chlorotic leaf tissue (Fig. 62g).
Rhytisma salicinum (Pers.:Fr.) Fr.	willow	Black stromata with raised centers 2-5 mm diameter form on upper leaf surfaces (Fig. 62h).
Taphrina populi-salicis Mix	cottonwood, willow	Golden-yellow leaf spots (Fig. 62i).
Uncinula bicornis (Wallr.:Fr.) Lév	maple	Powdery white mycelium appears on leaf surface(s) in late summer and fall (Fig. 62j).

References:

Funk, A. 1985. Foliar fungi of western trees. Can. For. Serv., Inf. Rep. BC-X-265.

Figure 62f: Leaf spots on hybrid poplar caused by *Mycosphaerella populicola*. Figure 62g: Stromata of *Rhytisma punctatum* on bigleaf maple. Figure 62h: Stromata of *Rhytisma salicinum* on willow.
Figure 62i: Leaf spots caused by *Taphrina populina* (similar to *Taphrina populi-salicis)* on cottonwood.
Figure 62j: *Uncinula bicornis* on bigleaf maple.

Mistletoes

Dwarf Mistletoes

Arceuthobium spp.

Dicotyledoneae, Viscaceae, Loranthaceae

Dwarf mistletoes are parasitic flowering plants that grow on stems and branches of living conifers. They depend almost entirely on their hosts for support, water, and nutrition. Both male and female plants are generally produced on the same host, but arising from separate infections. Following fertilization, the female plant produces green to dark brown-purple berries from which the mature seeds are forcibly ejected for distances up to 15 m. The seeds, covered with a sticky, mucilaginous pulp, must germinate on and penetrate the bark of a susceptible host to survive. After penetration, a system of root-like strands and perennial sinkers develops in the inner bark. The sinkers ultimately come in contact with and become embedded in the woody tissues of the tree causing distortion of the annual rings and swelling of bark and wood tissues. Aerial shoots, buds and flowers usually develop within 3 years of initial infection. Dwarf mistletoe shoots vary in size, for example, those of Douglas-fir dwarf mistletoe are only about 2.5 cm long whereas lodgepole pine dwarf mistletoe may be as long as 12 cm.

Hosts: Most dwarf mistletoe species are host-specific, occurring primarily on one species of conifer. Many dwarf mistletoe species will spread from the preferred hosts to other conifer species when they are growing in close proximity. Western redcedar, yellow cedar, western yew, and juniper appear to be immune from infection but all other native conifers in B.C. are susceptible to attack.

Identification: Conspicuous broom symptoms caused by localized branch proliferation are associated with most mistletoe species. The size and extent of brooms varies among hosts (Figs. 63a-f). Where brooms are observed, branches should be checked for the presence of aerial dwarf mistletoe shoots to distinguish broom symptoms caused by other pathogens (e.g., Elytroderma needle cast) or physiological disorders. Branches and stems are often swollen at the site of dwarf mistletoe infections (Fig. 63g). Aerial shoots of the dwarf mistletoe plants vary in size (typically 5-8 cm high), colour (usually greenish-yellow), and pattern of branching (Figs. 63h, 63i). For example, Douglas-fir dwarf mistletoe plants are often small and inconspicuous (Fig. 63j), larch dwarf mistletoe shoots are purple or green, and those of lodgepole pine dwarf mistletoe are arranged in a whorled pattern, distinguishing them from all other species. Basal cups remain after aerial shoots are shed in the fall (Fig. 63j). Mistletoe brooms develop from either systemic infections or as a result of discrete, localized infections. On brooms formed from systemic infections, aerial shoot, and basal cups are found near the tips of branches. On local-infection brooms, these structures are only found near the original site of infection.

Damage: Heavy infections reduce wood quality, diameter and height growth, and sometimes result in the death of the tree. Dead tissues resulting from the parasitic action of the dwarf mistletoe plant provide entrance points for stain and decay producing fungi. Infected branches frequently break due to decay or broom size, presenting a hazard in high-use recreational sites (Fig. 63k).

Remarks: Since the external structures of dwarf mistletoes are generally not visible for 2-3 years after infection, surveys for mistletoe must consider these latent infections. The aerial shoots of the dwarf mistletoe plant are sometimes attacked by insects and fungi. A common fungal parasite, *Wallrothiella arceuthobium* (Peck) Sacc., produces clusters of black fruiting bodies at the tips

Figures 63a-62f: Broom symptoms of dwarf mistletoe species; 63a, 63b: Douglas-fir dwarf mistletoe, 63c: Larch dwarf mistletoe, 63d, 63e: Lodgepole pine dwarf mistletoe, 63f: Hemlock dwarf mistletoe.

of the female flowers, inhibiting the development of the fruit and seed. Some scientists treat all dwarf mistletoes found in B.C. as one species, *Arceuthobium campylopodum* Engelmann in Gray, but this book follows the taxonomic system of Hawksworth and Weins (1995), assigning names according to host-specificity.

Dwarf mistletoe species	Hosts	Geographic distribution
Douglas-fir dwarf mistletoe *Arceuthobium douglasii* Engelmann	Found mainly on Douglas-fir, occasionally on grand fir and Engelmann spruce.	In B.C., Douglas-fir mistletoe is restricted to the southern interior. It does not occur west of the Cascades in B.C., Washington, or Oregon.
Larch dwarf mistletoe *Arceuthobium laricis* (Piper) St. John	The preferred host is western larch, occasionally found on western white, ponderosa, and lodge-pole pine, subalpine and grand fir, and Engelmann spruce.	Larch dwarf mistletoe is found in the southeast interior of the province following the range of western larch.
Lodgepole pine dwarf mistletoe *Arceuthobium americanum* Nutt. ex Engelmann	Lodgepole pine is the preferred host, occasionally found on ponderosa pine and white and Engelmann spruce.	Lodgepole pine dwarf mistletoe is found throughout the range of lodgepole pine in the interior of B.C.
Hemlock dwarf mistletoe *Arceuthobium tsugense* (Rosendahl) Jones	Western and mountain hemlock are the preferred hosts, occasionally found on lodgepole pine, amabilis fir, rarely on grand and subalpine fir, Sitka and Englemann spruce, and western white pine.	Hemlock dwarf mistletoe is restricted to the range of coastal western hemlock. It is not found in the interior of B.C.

References:

Van Sickle, G. A. and R. B. Smith. 1978. Dwarf mistletoe controls in British Columbia. *In* USFS Gen. Tech. Rep. PSW-31. pp. 106-111.

Hawksworth, F. G. and D. Wiens. 1995. Dwarf mistletoe: biology, pathology, and systematics. USDA For. Serv. Agric. Hdbk. No. 450.

Unger, L. 1992. Dwarf mistletoes. Can. For. Serv., Forest Pest Leaf. No. 44. Victoria, B.C.

Figure 63g: Stem swelling associated with lodgepole pine dwarf mistletoe. Figure 63h: Aerial shoots and berries of lodgepole pine dwarf mistletoe. Figure 63i: Aerial shoots and berries of larch dwarf mistletoe. Note purple colour of shoots. Figure 63j: Small aerial shoots and basal cups of Douglas-fir dwarf mistletoe. Figure 63k: Broken branch due to a heavy broom of hemlock dwarf mistletoe on western hemlock.

Non-Infectious Diseases

Basal and Trunk Scars

Scars found on the bole of trees are caused by a number of agents; consequently, associated symptoms may be variable. Charring indicates a fire origin; extensive scars associated with broken and missing branches suggest damage caused by falling trees; and scars encompassing branches indicate animal or fungus attack. Logging activities frequently result in tree scars, which are usually irregular in outline, sometimes deeply gouged and most frequently near the base of the tree (Fig. 64a). Various diseases, notably Armillaria root rot, are also responsible for basal lesions. Direct loss from scarring is usually small; however, if the wood becomes infected with stain or wood decaying fungi, the indirect loss may be substantial (Fig. 64b).

Frost Injury

Frost injury usually results from a sudden drop in air temperature before plant tissues have hardened-off. Localized lesions are formed when the bark and cambium are killed. Eventually, the dead tissues covering the lesion are sloughed-off exposing the sapwood. Several years may be required before the lesion is callused over. During this period the exposed wood acts as an entrance court for wood decay fungi capable of causing extensive damage to the heartwood. All tree species are susceptible to this damage.

Frost cracks (Fig. 64c) are formed when there is a pronounced drop in temperature during the dormant period of tree growth. The inner wood remains comparatively warm while the outer wood becomes cold and contracts rapidly causing cracks or splits in the trunk. Repeated opening of the cracks by cold temperatures or trunk movement results in considerable callus tissue growth that frequently appears as black raised lines on the stem. Frost cracks provide entrance courts for wood decay fungi and as such may result in significant damage.

Sunscald

Sunscald is caused by the intense heat of direct sunrays. Damaged areas on the main stem, usually on the southwest side of the tree, are initially copper to bright red, standing out in marked contrast to adjacent healthy bark. These colours are not persistent and it may be difficult after a period of time to recognize previously damaged tissues. In severe cases, the bark in affected areas dies and sloughs off. Rapidly growing trees and trees suddenly exposed to strong sunlight, as may occur following thinning or pruning, appear to be most susceptible. There is thought to be no permanent injury unless the bark is killed creating open scars through which wood decay fungi can gain entrance to susceptible tissues.

Winter Kill

Although very low temperatures are required to kill trees, particularly if they are established on good sites, temperatures just below freezing are sufficient to damage foliage that has not hardened-off. Foliage may also be killed when exposed to warm, drying winds when the ground is still frozen because the trees are unable to replace the water lost through transpiration; the needles become desiccated, turn red and die (Fig. 64d). In mountainous areas injury may be confined to an altitudinal zone corresponding to the pathway of drying winds, hence the common name "red belt." Height and diameter growth are retarded and damaged trees are weakened and predisposed to attack by other agents.

Figure 64a: Large stem scar resulting from logging injury. Figure 64b: Decay in western larch associated with a 10-year-old injury. Figure 64c: Frost crack on subalpine fir.
Figure 64d: Drought mortality in lodgepole pine and Douglas-fir.

Abiotic Diseases

Cedar Flagging

Although not a disease, reference is made to cedar flagging because of interest in its cause and significance. Flagging is a normal condition in western redcedar; branchlets die during the dry, hot portion of the summer and toward the end of the growing season. It is recognized by the occurrence of isolated dying or dead, yellow or red branchlets (Fig. 64e). The condition is not believed to have a detrimental effect on tree growth. Cedar flagging could be confused with discoloured foliar symptoms caused by cedar leaf blight (*Didymascella thujina*). The fungal disease can be distinguished by its scattered foliar symptoms and the presence of fruiting bodies, when present.

Top Killing

Top killing of trees may be caused by fungi, insects, or adverse climatic disturbances. Killing by low temperatures is most likely to occur in exposed areas, such as ridges, or in frost pockets. Drought injury is generally prevalent on sites of low moisture-holding capacity; shoot dieback may be progressive if the moisture deficiency is severe and prolonged, appearing first in the upper crown, and generally extending downward. The first signs of drought damage to broadleaf foliage are wilting, followed by browning and drying from the margins inward (Fig. 64f). Fungi may attack the weakened and dead portions of a tree, extending damage to adjacent tissues.

Chemical and Fume Injury

A number of man-made chemicals in the form of gases (SO_2, other atmospheric pollutants) or liquids (pesticide sprays, acid rain, road salt spray) can be damaging to trees. When trees are injured by noxious industrial fumes, the foliage absorbs the gases for a prolonged period before the injury becomes apparent. Symptoms and severity of damage vary among trees species, concentration and type of gas, duration of exposure, and distance from the source of the fumes. Generally, necrosis of conifer needles starts at the tips (Fig. 64g), while broadleaf foliage is affected first in the tissues between the veins, giving the leaf a mottled appearance (Fig. 64h). Foliage buds, branches, and entire trees may be killed, the damage sometimes occurring over extensive areas. Damage from salt spray is common on foliage in areas where salt is applied to roads in the winter (Fig. 64i).

Figure 64e: Cedar flagging. Figure 64f: Foliar symptoms on black cottonwood due to moisture deficit. Figure 64g: Air pollution damage to spruce. Figure 64h: SO₂ damage to red alder leaves.

Top Breakage

In young trees, broken tops, attributable to snow, ice, and wind, and to injuries caused by animals and insects, result in double or multiple leaders (Fig. 64j). This is not usually of consequence for, unless a tree is affected repeatedly, one of the leaders will assume dominance and the reduction in height growth will be negligible. In older trees top breakage is usually attributable to the action of ice and snow. Breakage in stems greater than 10 cm diameter frequently serve as entrance courts for wood decay fungi and substantial volumes of timber can be lost.

Sapsucker Damage

Sapsuckers are only one of several groups of birds that cause tree damage. When feeding they puncture the bark in definite patterns, for example, partial rings around tree limbs or uniform vertical rows on the main stem (Fig. 64k). These punctures serve as entry points for stain or decay producing fungi.

Flooding

When the soil surrounding tree roots becomes waterlogged, roots are often killed resulting in tree death (Fig. 64l). Trees damaged through flooding may be more susceptible to infection by fungal pathogens. Different tree species tolerate flooding to different degrees, for example, alder, willow, poplar, lodgepole pine, and black spruce can survive in soils that are periodically flooded, whereas white and Sitka spruce are more sensitive.

Figure 64i: Roadside salt damage to Douglas-fir. Figure 64j: Snow damage to young aspen.
Figure 64k: Sapsucker feeding scars. Figure 64l: Trees killed by flooding.

Common and Latin Names of Host Plants

The common names used in this book follow Brako *et al.*(1995). Where discrepancies occur regarding locally accepted common names, Pojar and MacKinnon *et al.*(1994) and MacKinnon, Pojar, and Coupe (1992) are followed. Latin names follow Farr *et al.* (1989).

Acacia	*Acacia koa* A. Grey
Alder	
mountain alder	*Alnus tenuifolia* Nutt.
red alder	*Alnus rubra* Bong.
Sitka alder	*Alnus sinuata* (Regel) Rydb.
Amelanchier	*Amelanchier* Medik.
apple	*Malus domestica* Borkh.
crabapple	*Malus sylvestris* Mill.
arbutus	*Arbutus menziesii* Pursh
Arctostaphylos	*Arctostaphylos* Adans.
Aspen	
trembling aspen	*Populus tremuloides* Michx.
basswood	*Tilia americana* L.
bastard toadflax	*Geocaulon lividum* (Richardson) Fernald
beech	*Fagus* L.
Birch	
paper birch	*Betula papyrifera* Marsh.
water birch	*Betula occidentalis* Hook.
white birch	*Betula papyrifera* Marsh.
yellow birch	*Betula alleghaniensis* Britton
blackberry	*Rubus* L.
Blueberry	
oval-leaf blueberry	*Vaccinium ovalifolium* Sm.
velvet-leaf blueberry	*Vaccinium myrtilloides* Michx.
bracted lousewort	*Pedicularis bracteosa* Benth.
buckthorn	*Rhamnus* L.
	Rhamnus cathartica L.
Camellia	*Camellia sasanqua* Thunb.
Cedar	
California incense cedar	*Calocedrus decurrens* (Torr.) Florin
incense cedar	*Calocedrus decurrens* (Torr.) Florin
Port Orford cedar	*Chamaecyparis lawsoniana* (A. Murray.) Parl.
western redcedar	*Thuja plicata* Donn ex D. Don
yellow cedar	*Chamaecyparis nootkatensis* (D. Don) Spach
Cercocarpus	*Cercocarpus* spp. Kunth
Chamaecyparis	*Chamaecyparis thyoides* (L.) Britton *et al.*
Cherry	*Prunus* L.
bitter cherry	*Prunus emarginata* (Hook.) Walp.
chokecherry	*Prunus virginiana* L.
Chestnut	*Castanea* spp. Mill.
horse chestnut	*Aesculus* spp. L.

chickweed	*Cerastium* spp. L.
Choisya	*Choisya* spp. Kunth in H. B. K.
Cotoneaster	*Cotoneaster* spp. Medik.
Cottonwood	
black cottonwood	*Populus trichocarpa* Torr. & A. Grey
eastern cottonwood	*Populus deltoides* Marsh.
lanceleaf cottonwood	*Populus* x *acuminata* Rydb.
Fremont's poplar	*Populus fremontii* S. Watson
cow-wheat	*Melampyrum lineare* Desr.
currant	*Ribes* L.
Diospyros	*Diospyros virginiana* L.
Dogwood	
Pacific dogwood	*Cornus nuttalli* Audubon
Douglas-fir	*Pseudotsuga menziesii* (Mirb.) Franco
dwarf bilberry	*Vaccinium caespitosum* Michx.
elm	*Ulmus* spp. L.
eucalyptus	*Eucalyptus cinerea* F. Muell. ex Benth.
fig	*Ficus* spp. L.
fir	
alpine fir	*Abies lasiocarpa* (Hook.) Nutt.
Amabilis fir	*Abies amabilis* Douglas ex Forbes
California red fir	*Abies magnifica* A. Murray bis
grand fir (balsam)	*Abies grandis* (Douglas ex D. Don) Lindl.
noble fir	*Abies procera* Rehder
Pacific silver fir	*Abies amabilis* Douglas ex Forbes
red fir	*Abies magnifica* A. Murray bis
subalpine fir	*Abies lasiocarpa* (Hook.) Nutt.
white fir	*Abies concolor* (Gordon & Glend.) Lindl. ex Hildebr.
fireweed	*Epilobium angustifolium* L.
fuschia	*Epilobium canum* (Greene) Raven
godetia	*Clarkia amoena* (Lehm.) A. Nels.
gooseberry	*Ribes* spp.L.
grape	*Vitis* spp. L.
grouseberry	*Vaccinium scoparium* Leiberg ex Crép.
hackberry	*Celtis* spp. L.
hazelnut	*Corylus* spp. L.
Hemlock	
eastern hemlock	*Tsuga canadensis* (L.) Carrière
mountain Hemlock	*Tsuga mertensiana* (Bong.) Carrière
western Hemlock	*Tsuga heterophylla* (Raf.) Sarg.
hickory	*Carya* spp. Nutt.
honey locust	*Gleditsia triacanthos* L.
honeysuckle	*Lonicera* L.
hornbeam	*Carpinus* spp. L.
Huckleberry	
black huckleberry	*Vaccinium membranaceum* Dougl. ex Hook.
evergreen huckleberry	*Vaccinium ovatum* Pursh
he-huckleberry	*Lyonia ligustrina* (L.) DC.

red huckleberry	*Vaccinium parvifolium* Sm.
ironwood	*Ostrya virginiana* (Mill.) K. Koch
Juniper	
Rocky Mountain juniper	*Juniperus scopulorum* Sarg.
Kalmia	*Kalmia latifolia* L.
kinnikinnick	*Arctostaphylos uva-ursi* (L.) Spreng.
Labrador-tea	*Ledum groenlandicum* Oeder.
northern Labrador-tea	*Ledum deumbens* (Ait.) Lodd.
Larch	
subalpine larch	*Larix lyallii* Parl.
European larch	*Larix decidua* Mill.
Japanese larch	*Larix kaempferi* (Lamb.) Carrière
western larch	*Larix occidentalis* Nutt.
lilac	*Syringa vulgaris* L.
lingonberry	*Vaccinium vitis-idaea* L.
locust	*Robinia* spp. L.
London planetree	*Platanus acerifolia* (Aiton) Willd.
magnolia	*Magnolia* spp. L.
Maple	
bigleaf maple	*Acer macrophyllum* Pursh
vine maple	*Acer circinatum* Pursh
mimosa	*Albizia julibrissin* Durazz.
mountain ash	*Sorbus americana* Marsh.
nectarine	*Prunus persica* (L.) Batsch var. *nucipersica* (Suckow) C.K. Schneid.
Oak	
Garry oak	*Quercus garryana* Douglas
Oregon boxwood	*Pachistima myrsinites* (Pursh) Raf.
paintbrush	*Castilleja* spp. Mutis ex L.f.
Pale Comandra	*Comandra pallida* A. DC.
peach	*Prunus persica* (L.) Batsch.
pear	*Pyrus communis* L.
plum	*Prunus* L.
Pine	
Austrian pine	*Pinus nigra* Arnold
bishop's pine	*Pinus muricata* D. Don
eastern white pine	*Pinus strobus* L.
European black pine	*Pinus nigra* Arnold
jack pine	*Pinus banksiana* Lamb.
limber pine	*Pinus flexilis* E. James
loblolly pine	*Pinus taeda* L.
lodgepole pine	*Pinus contorta* Dougl. & Loud.
maritime pine	*Pinus pinaster* Aiton
Monterey pine	*Pinus radiata* D. Don
mugo pine	*Pinus mugo* Turra
ponderosa pine	*Pinus ponderosa* Douglas ex P. Laws. & C. Laws.
red pine	*Pinus resinosa* Aiton
Scots pine	*Pinus sylvestris* L.

shortleaf pine	*Pinus echinata* Mill.
spruce pine	*Pinus glabra* Walter,
sugar pine	*Pinus lambertiana* Douglas
Swiss stone pine	*Pinus cembra* L.
Virginia pine	*Pinus virginiana* Mill.
western white pine	*Pinus monticola* Douglas ex D. Don
white bark pine	*Pinus albicaulis* Engelm.

Poplar

balsam poplar	*Populus balsamifera* L.
black poplar	*Populus nigra* L.
Lombardy poplar	*Populus nigra* L.
Purshia	*Purshia tridentata* (Pursh) DC.
quince	*Cydonia oblonga* Mill.
Rhododendron	*Rhododendron* spp. L.
sagebrush	*Artemisia tridentata* Nutt.
sandwort	*Arenaria* spp. L.
saskatoon	*Amelanchier alnifolia* (Nutt.) Nutt.
satinflower	*Clarkia amoena* (Lehm.) A. Nelson

Sequoia

coast redwood	*Sequioa sempervirens* (D. Don) Endl.
dawn redwood	*Metasequoia glyptostroboides* Hu & W.C. Cheng
giant sequoia	*Sequoiadendron giganteum* (Lindl.) Buchholz
single delight	*Moneses uniflora* (L.) A. Grey
Spirea	*Spirea* spp. L.

Spruce

black spruce	*Picea mariana* (Mill.) B.S.P.
Colorado spruce	*Picea pungens* Engelm.
Engelmann spruce	*Picea engelmannii* Parry ex Engelm.
Norway spruce	*Picea abies* (L.) H. Karst.
red spruce	*Picea rubens* Sarg.
Sitka spruce	*Picea sitchensis* (Bong.) Carrière
white spruce	*Picea glauca* (Moench) Voss
starwort	*Stellaria* spp. L
sweet fern	*Comptonia perigrina* (L.) J. M. Coulter
sweet gale	*Myrica gale* L.
sweet-gum	*Liquidamber styraciflua* L.
sycamore	*Platanus* spp. L.
tamarack	*Larix laricina* (Du Roi) K. Koch
tulip-tree	*Liriodendron tulipifera* L.
tupelo	*Nyssa* spp. L.
walnut	*Juglans* spp. L.
willow	*Salix* spp. L.
wintergreen	*Pyrola* spp. L.
yellow owl's clover	*Orthocarpus luteus* Nutt.
yellow-rattle	*Rhinanthus minor* L.

Yew

| western yew | *Taxus brevifolia* Nutt. |

Glossary

acute: pointed, sharp-edged, less than a right angle.

acyanophilous (cf. cyanophilous): not readily absorbing a blue stain such as cotton blue or gentian violet.

advanced decay: advanced destruction of plant or animal matter by fungi or other micro-organisms. Wood tissue is generally soft.

aecial host: host of a rust fungus on which spematia and aeciospores are formed.

aeciospore: binucleate asexual spores of rust fungi formed as a result of the sexual fusion of cells but not of the nuclei.

aecium (pl. -ia): site of production of aeciospores in the rust fungi.

alternate host: one or the other of the two unlike hosts of a heteroecious rust fungus.

amphigenous: growing all around or on both sides of a leaf or needle.

ampulliform: flask-shaped.

amyloid: spores and hyphae are designated as amyloid if they turn grey or blue-black upon treatment with Melzer's Iodine reagent (see dextrinoid, IKI-).

anamorph: imperfect state of a fungus, produces asexual spores (conidia)

annual: a plant that completes its life cycle within 1 year and then dies.

annulus: the ring of tissue left on the stalk (stipe) of a mushroom when the partial veil (pileus) breaks.

apiculus: a short projection at one end of a spore.

apothecium (pl. -ca): the cup or saucer-shaped fruiting body of the Ascomycotina.

arthroconidium (pl. -ia): an asexual spore produced from the division a hypha into separate cells.

aseptate: without crosswalls, generally referring to fungal hyphae.

ascus (pl. -ci): a sac-like cell of an Ascomycete within which two haploid nuclei fuse, after which three divisions occur, two of them meiotic, resulting in eight ascospores.

ascospore: a sexually generated propagative unit of the Ascomycotina, a spore produced within an ascus.

ascostroma (pl. -mata): a stroma containing asci.

asexual stage (cf. sexual stage): that part of a life cycle where reproduction does not involve the fusion of gametes and meiosis.

bacillar: rod-like in form.

basidiospore: a propagative cell of the Basidiomycotina containing one or two haploid nuclei produced, after meiosis, on a basidium.

bilabiate: from the Latin two-lipped, describing a dehiscence mechanism in bitunicate asci where the tip of the ascus splits to form two lips

biseriate: arranged in or having two series or rows.

bitunicate: having two walls, as in the asci of Loculoascomycetes.

callus: wound tissue, composed of soft parenchymatous tissue formed on or about injured surfaces of stems and roots.

cambium: a persistent layer of generative, meristematic cells that gives rise to secondary wood (xylem) and secondary inner bark (phloem).

canker: a disease of woody plants characterized by sharply delimited necrosis of the cortical tissues and malformation of the bark caused by recurring localized killing of the cambium layer.

caulicolous: living on herbaceous stems.

chlamydospore: an asexual spore (primarily for survival, not dissemination) formed by modification of a hyphal segment.

chlorosis (adj. chlorotic): an unseasonable yellowing of the foliage, symptomatic of a chlorophyll deficiency in the leaf tissues.

circumscissile: opening or cracking along a circle.

clamp connection (also clamp): a bridge-like hyphal connection characteristic of the secondary mycelium of many Basidiomycetes.

clavate: club-like, narrowed at the base.

clypeus: a shield-like growth over a perithecium.

concolorous: of one colour

conidium (pl. -ia): an asexual fungal spore.

conidiophores: a specialized hypha from which conidia are produced.

conk: a fruiting body of a wood-destroying fungus.

context: the inner or body tissue of a fruiting body that supports the fruiting surface.

cyanophilous (cf. acyanophilous): readily absorbing a blue stain such as cotton blue or gentian violet.

cystidium (pl. -ia): a sterile structure, frequently of distinctive shape, generally occurring on the hymenial surface of a basidiomycete fruiting body.

daedaloid: pores that are irregularly lobed and sinuous in outline, labyrinthiform.

dextrinoid: spores and hyphae are designated as dextrinoid if they turn reddish-brown upon treatment with Melzer's Iodine reagent (see amyloid, IKI-).

dieback: the progressive dying, from the tip downward, of twigs, branches, tops, or roots of plants.

echinulate: covered with slender sharp spines, here referring to spore surface characteristics.

effused-reflexed: spread out over the substratum and turned back at the margin; refers to the growth form of polypore fruiting bodies.

epidemic: a widespread high level of disease incidence beyond normal proportions.

epidermis: a superficial layer of cells occurring on all parts of the primary plant body; stems, leaves, roots, flowers, and seeds.

epiphyllous: growing on the upper, adaxial surface of a leaf or needle.

episporium (also epispore): the thick fundamental layer that determines the shape of the spore.

erumpent: bursting through the bark.

excipulum: tissues of the apothecium; ectal-, forms outermost layers, including the margin, and medullary-, the zone enclosed by the ectal excipulum and the hypothecium.

filiform: thread-like.

flag (also flagging): a dying, or recently dead, twig or branch, the foliage of which contrasts in colour with the normal green foliage of living trees.

fruiting body (also sporophore, conk): a structure that bears the spore-producing structures and spores in fleshy and woody higher fungi.

fungus (pl. -gi): one group of the lower plants that lack chlorophyll, thus requiring a host from which to obtain food.

fusoid: almost fusiform.

fusiform: spindle shaped, tapering at both ends.

generative hyphae: the hyphal type present in all basidiocarps, typically thin-walled, with clamps or simple-septate; from them develop the hymenial elements, and in some species, the skeletal and binding hyphae.

geniculate: bent like a knee.

germ pore: a thin circular area in the spore wall through which the germ tube develops.

guttulate: having one or more oil drops inside.

heartwood: the central part of a tree that is no longer active in the transport or storage of water or nutrients.

host: a plant or other organism that furnishes subsistence to, or harbours, a parasite.

hypha (pl. -ae): a fungal thread or filament.

hyaline: transparent, colourless.

hymenium: the spore bearing layer of a fungal fruiting structure.

hyperparasite (adj. -itic): a parasite that is parasitic on another parasite.

hypertrophy: the state of having growth greater than normal.

hypophyllous: growing on the lower, abaxial surface of a leaf or needle.

hypothecium: the hyphal layer under the hymenium of an apothecium.

hysterothecium (pl. -cia): an elongated ascocarp with an longitudinal slit; characteristic of some needle-cast fungi.

IKI-: no colour response when treated with Melzer's Iodine reagent; sometimes referred to as inamyloid (see amyloid, dextrinoid).

incipient decay: an early stage in decay in which the wood may show discoloration but is not otherwise visibly altered. The wood is generally firm and sound.

indeterminate: having the edge not well defined, especially of fruiting-bodies and leaf-spots; continuing growth indefinitely.

infection court: the site of invasion of a host by a pathogen.

inoculum: spores or tissue of a pathogen that serve to initiate disease in a plant.

intercalary: between apex and base.

J-: does not stain in iodine; common usage in Ascomycete identification.

laccate: polished, varnished, shining.

laminate: separated into sheets or layers (lamellae).

lenticular: like a double convex lens in form.

lesion: a definite, localized area of dead tissue, a circumscribed diseased area.

locule: a cavity in a stroma.

Melzer's reagent: a solution consisting of 2.5 g iodine, 7.5 g potassium iodide, and 100 g chloral hydrate per 100 mL of water used to detect amyloid and dextrinoid reactions.

monostichous: forming in a line; refers here to the alignment of ascospores in as ascus.

mycelial fan: a fan-shaped mycelial mat forming under the bark of roots and lower stems of trees; often associated with Armillaria root rot.

mycelium: collective term for hyphae or fungus filaments.

necrosis: death of the affected tissues.

obligate parasite: a parasite that is incapable of existing independently of living tissues.

ostiole: a pore through which spores are freed from a perithecium or pycnidium.

papillate: small, rounded.

paraphyses: sterile structures in a hymenium.

parasite: an organism that draws a part or the whole of its nourishment from another living organism.

parenchyma: tissue composed of more or less isodiametric cells, usually thin-walled with inter-cellular spaces (cf. pseudoparenchyma).

pathogen: an organism capable of causing disease.

pathogenic: disease-causing or able to be so.

penicillate: like a little brush.

perennial: an organism that lives from year-to-year.

peridium (pl. -ia): the wall or limiting membrane of a sporangium or other fungal fruiting structure

periderm: the outermost, corky layer of bark of a tree.

peridermioid: more or less like the peridermium.

peridermium (pl. -ia): an aecium with a blister-like, tongue-shaped, or cylindrical peridium.

perithecium: the sub-globose or flask-shaped ascocarp of an Ascomycete fungus.

phloem: food-conducting tissue, consisting of sieve tubes, companion cells, phloem parenchyma, and fibers.

phialide (adj. phialidic): a type of conidiogenous cell that produces conidia through a special opening where neither wall contributes toward formation of the conidium; conidia are produced basipetally with no detectable increase in length.

plectenchyma: fungal tissue formed by hyphae becoming twisted and fixed together.

pore: an opening on the fertile surface of bolete and polypore fungi, through which basidiospores are disseminated.

pore surface: the surface of polypore or bolete fruiting body bearing pores through with basidiospores are disseminated.

poroid: with pores.

pseudooperculum: characteristic of one of nine structural types of ascus (pseudooperculate).

pseudoparaphyses: sterile hyphal structures connected to both the upper and lower surface of and ascocarp.

pseudoparenchyma: plant tissue composed of more or less isodiametric cells.

punk knot: decayed branch stubs that often indicate the presence of decay in a tree.

pustule: a blister-like, frequently erumpent, spot or spore-mass.

pycnidium: a flask-shaped, asexual fruiting body lined with conidiophores.

pyriform: pear-shaped.

resinosis: an abnormal exudation of resin or pitch from conifers.

resupinate: a fruiting body reclined or flat on the substratum.

reverse: refers to the colour of the bottom of a petri plate on which a fungal culture is growing.

rhizomorph: a strand or cord of compact mycelium, often dark coloured; characteristic of *Armillaria* spp.

rugulose: delicately wrinkled.

semipileate: with a cap that is partially appressed to the substrate.

saprophyte: an organism using dead organic material as food.

septate: possessing a cross-wall forming a division in a spore or hypha.

seta: a stiff hair or bristle.

sexual stage (cf. asexual stage): that part of a life cycle where reproduction involves the fusion of gametes and meiosis.

sign: visible evidence of a disease organism, (e.g., mycelium, fruiting bodies).

skeletal hyphae: thick-walled hyphae, branched or unbranched, aseptate, straight or slightly flexuous with thin-walled apices.

spermatium (pl. -ia): non-motile, uninucleate, spore-like male structure serving as a gamete in sexual reproduction.

spermagonium (pl. -ia): a fruiting structure in which spermatia are produced, sometimes referred to as a pycnium in some rust fungus literature.

spore: the reproductive structure of fungi and other cryptograms, corresponding to a seed in flowering plants.

sporodochium (pl. -ia): a cushion-shaped conidial fruiting structure in which the spore mass is supported by a stroma covered by short conidiophores.

sporophore: see fruiting body.

sterigma (pl. -ata): a tapering projection on a basidium on which basidiospores develop.

sterile conk: a conk not producing spores or a sporocarp.

stipe: a stalk-like or stem-like structure that supports the pileus of a basidiomycete fruiting body.

stipitate: possessing a stipe.

stroma (pl. -ata): a mass or matrix of vegetative hyphae, with or without tissue of the host or substrate, sometimes sclerotium-like in form, in or on which spores are produced.

subcuticular: underlying the cuticle.

subhypodermal: underlying the hypodermis.

subiculum: a net-like, or crust-like growth of mycelium from which fruiting bodies are formed.

subulate: tapering to a point; awl-shaped.

symptom: the noticeable evidence of change in the physiology or morphology of a host as a result of disease.

systemic: a parasite which spreads throughout the host; a fungicide that is absorbed by the roots and is translocated to other parts of the plant.

teleomorph: perfect state of a fungus, produces sexual spores (ascospores, basidiospores)

telial host: host of a rust fungus on which urediniospores, teliospores and basidiospores are formed.

telium (pl. -ia): a sorus producing teliospores; refers to rust fungi.

teliospore: a spore (commonly a winter or resting spore) of the rust fungi from which the basidium is produced.

terminal vesicle: the swollen apex of the conidiophore or hypha.

tramal hyphae: the layer of hyphae in the central part of a lamella of an agaric, a spine of Hydnaceae, or the partition between pores in a polyphore.

tuberculate: having tubercles, having small wart-like processes.

tubes: spore-bearing structures in polypores and boletes, aligned vertically and terminating in openings on the pore surface.

uniseriate: arranged in or having one series or row.

urediniospore: a binucleate spore borne in a uredinium and capable of infecting the same host on which it originated, usually echinulate.

uredinium (pl. -ia): a sorus that produces urediniospores, produced after the aecium and after the telium in the life cycle of rust fungi.

verruculose: possessing delicate, small rounded processes or warts.

verticillate: having parts in rings (verticils), whorled.

virulence: degree of pathogenicity of a pathogen, the relative capacity of a pathogen to cause disease.

xylem: a plant tissue consisting of tracheids, vessels, parenchyma cells and fibers; wood.

zone lines: narrow, dark-brown or black lines in decayed wood, generally resulting from the interaction of different strains or species of fungi.

General References

Brako, L., A. Y. Rossman, and D. F. Farr. 1995. Scientific and common names of 7,000 vascular plants in the United States. APS Press. St. Paul, MN.

Farr, D. F., G. F. Bills, G. P. Chamuris, and A. Y. Rossman. 1989. Fungi on plants and plant products in the United States. APS Press. St. Paul, MN.

Funk, A. 1985. Foliar fungi of western trees. Can. For. Serv., Inf. Rep. BC-X-265.

Gilbertson, R. L. and L. Ryvarden. 1986. North American Polypores. (Vol 1) Fungiflora, Oslo.

Gilbertson, R. L. and L. Ryvarden. 1987. North American Polypores. (Vol 2) Fungiflora, Oslo.

Hawksworth, F. G., R. L. Gilbertson, and G. W. Wallis. 1985. Common names for tree diseases in the western United States and western Canada. Suppl. Proc. 32nd Annual Western International Forest Disease Work Conference.

Nobles, M. K. 1948. Studies in forest pathology VI. Identification of cultures of wood-rotting fungi. Can. J. For. Res., Sec. C., Bot. Sci. 20: 281-431.

MacKinnon, A., J. Pojar, and R. Coupé. 1992. Plants of Northern British Columbia. Lone Pine Press. Edmonton.

Pojar, J., and A. MacKinnon. 1994. Plants of Coastal British Columbia. Lone Pine Press. Edmonton.

Stalpers, J. A. 1978. Identification of wood-inhabiting Aphyllophorales in pure culture. Centralb. Schimelc. Stud. Mycol. 16: 1-248.

Ziller, W. G. 1974. The tree rusts of western Canada. Can. For. Serv., Publ. 1329. Victoria, B.C.

Host - Fungus Index

This index lists the disease organisms found on the important commercial tree species of B.C. Names in **bold-face** indicate that the organism is very common to that particular host. These designations are based on the experience of the authors and other experts.

Red Alder
(*Alnus rubra* Bong.)

Root Diseases
Armillaria ostoyae
Armillaria sinapina
Armillaria gallica
Armillaria cepistipes
Armillaria nabsnona
Heterobasidion annosum

Heart Rots
Fomes fomentarius
Fomitopsis pinicola
Ganoderma applanatum
Perenniporia subacida
Phellinus igniarius
Phellinus pini
Stereum sanguinolentum

Sap Rots
Chondrostereum purpureum
Gleopyllum sepiarium

Canker Diseases
Didymosphaeria oregonensis
Hypoxylon mammatum
Inonotus obliquus
Nectria cinnabarina
Nectria ditissima

Trembling Aspen
(*Populus tremuloides* Michx.)

Root Diseases
Armillari ostoyae
Armillaria sinapina
Heterobasidion annosum

Heart Rots
Fomitopsis pinicola
Ganoderma applanatum
Laetiporus sulphureus
Phellinus tremulae

Sap Rots
Chondrostereum purpureum
Gleopyllum sepiarium

Canker Diseases
Cytospora chrysosperma
Hypoxylon mammatum

Broadleaf Foliar Diseases
Ciborinia whetzelii
Drepanopezziza populorum
Marssonina populi
Melampsora albertensis
Mycosphaerella populicola
Septoria populicola
Venturia macularis

Bigleaf Maple
(*Acer macrophyllum* Pursh)

Root Diseases
Armillaria ostoyae
Armillaria sinapina
Armillaria gallica
Armillaria nabsnona
Heterobasidion annosum

Heart Rots
Fomitopsis pinicola
Ganoderma applanatum

Sap Rots
Chondrostereum purpureum

Broadleaf Foliar Diseases
Rhytisma punctatum
Uncinula bicornis

Birch
(*Betula papyrifera* Marsh.)

Root Diseases
Armillaria ostoyae

Armillaria sinapina
Armillaria cepistipes
Armillaria nabsnona
Phaeolus schweinitzii

Heart Rots
Fomes fomentarius
Fomitopsis pinicola
Ganoderma applanatum
Laetiporus sulphureus
Perenniporia subacida
Phellinus igniarius
Phellinus pini
Piptoporus betulinus

Sap Rots
Chondrostereum purpureum
Gleopyllum sepiarium

Canker Diseases
Inonotus obliquus
Nectria cinnabarina

Cottonwood
(**Populus trichocarpa** Torr. & A. Gray)

Root Diseases
Armillaria ostoyae
Armillaria sinapina
Armillaria nabsnona
Heterobasidion annosum

Heart Rots
Fomes fomentarius
Fomitopsis pinicola
Ganoderma applanatum
Perenniporia subacida
Phellinus igniarius
Pholiota populnea
Spongipellis delectans

Sap Rots
Chondrostereum purpureum
Gleopyllum sepiarium

Canker Diseases
Nectria cinnabarina

Broadleaf Foliar Diseases
Ciborinia whetzelii

Drepanopeziza populorum
Linospora tetraspora
Marssonina populi
Melampsora occidentalis
Mycosphaerella populicola
Septoria populicola
Taphrina populi-salicis
Venturia populina

Willow
(**Salix** sp.L.)

Root Diseases
Armillaria ostoyae
Armillaria sinapina
Armillaria nabsnona

Heart Rots
Fomes fomentarius
Fomitopsis pinicola
Ganoderma applanatum
Laetiporus sulphureus
Phellinus igniarius

Sap Rots
Chondrostereum purpureum
Gleopyllum sepiarium

Canker Diseases
Cytospora chrysosperma
Hypoxylon mammatum
Nectria cinnabarina

Broadleaf Foliar Diseases
Melampsora epitea
Melampsora abieti-capraearum
Melampsora epitea f. sp. tsugae
Melampsora paradoxa
Melampsora ribesii-purpureae
Rhytisma salicinum
Taphrina populi-salicis

Douglas-fir
(**Pseudotsuga menziesii** (Mirb.) Franco)

Root Diseases
Armillaria ostoyae
Armillaria sinapina

Heterobasidion annosum
Inonotus tomentosus
Leptographium wageneri
Phaeolus schweinitzii
Phellinus weirii
Rhizina undulata

Heart Rots
Ceriporiopsis rivulosa
Echinodontium tinctorium
Fomes fomentarius
Fomitopsis officinalis
Fomitopsis pinicola
Ganoderma applanatum
Hericium abietis
Laetiporus sulphureus
Perenniporia subacida
Phellinus hartigii
Phellinus igniarius
Phellinus pini
Postia sericeomollis
Stereum sanguinolentum
Veluticeps fimbriata

Sap Rots
Chondrostereum purpureum
Cryptoporus volvatus
Gleophyllum sepiarium
Trichaptum abeitinum

Canker Diseases
Diaporthe lokoyae

Conifer Rust Diseases
Needle
Melampsora albertensis
Melampsora occidentalis

Conifer Needle Diseases
Herpotrichia juniperi
Rhabdocline pseudotsugae

Dwarf Mistletoes
Arceuthobium douglasii (primary host)

Hemlock
Mountain Hemlock
(*Tsuga mertensiana* (Bong.) Carrière)

Root Diseases
Armillaria ostoyae

Armillaria sinapina
Heterobasidion annosum
Leptographium wageneri
Phaeolus schweinitzii
Phellinus weirii

Heart Rots
Echinodontium tinctorium
Fomitopsis officinalis
Fomitopsis pinicola
Ganoderma applanatum
Hericium abietis
Perenniporia subacida
Phellinus pini
Stereum sanguinolentum
Veluticeps fimbriata

Sap Rots
Gleophyllum sepiarium
Trichaptum abietinum

Conifer Rust Diseases
Stem and Broom
Naohidemyces vaccinii
Needle
Melampsora albertensis (inoculation only)
Melampsora epitea

Conifer Needle Diseases
Herpotrichia juniperi

Dwarf Mistletoes
Arceuthobium tsugense (primary host)

Western Hemlock
(*Tsuga heterophylla* (Raf.) Sarg.)

Root Diseases
Armillaria ostoyae
Armillaria sinapina
Heterobasidion annosum
Inonotus tomentosus
Leptographium wageneri
Phaeolus schweinitzii
Phellinus weirii
Rhizina undulata

Heart Rots
Ceriporiopsis rivulosa
Echinodontium tinctorium

Fomitopsis officinalis
Fomitopsis pinicola
Ganoderma applanatum
Hericium abietis
Laetiporus sulphureus
Neolentinus kauffmanii
Perenniporia subacida
Phellinus hartigii
Phellinus igniarius
Phellinus pini
Postia sericeomollis
Stereum sanguinolentum
Veluticeps fimbriata

Sap Rots
Chondrostereum purpureum
Cryptoporus volvatus
Gleophyllum sepiarium
Trichaptum abietinum

Canker Diseases
Diaporthe lokoyae
Nectria cinnabarina

Conifer Rust Diseases
Stem and Broom
Naohidemyces vaccinii
Needle
Melampsora epitea

Conifer Needle Diseases
Herpotrichia juniperi

Dwarf Mistletoes
Arceuthobium tsugense (primary host)

Juniper
(*Juniperus* L.)

Root Diseases
Armillaria ostoyae
Heterobasidion annosum

Heart Rots
Perenniporia subacida
Phellinus pini
Postia sericeomollis

Sap Rots
Gleophyllum sepiarium
Trichaptum abietinum

Pine
Lodgepole Pine
(*Pinus contorta* Douglas & Loud. var *latifolia* Engelm *ex* S. Wats.)

Root Diseases
Armillaria ostoyae
Armillaria sinapina
Heterobasidion annosum
Inonotus tomentosus
Leptographium wageneri
Phaeolus schweinitzii
Phellinus weirii
Rhizina undulata

Heart Rots
Fomitopsis officinalis
Fomitopsis pinicola
Laetiporus sulphureus
Perenniporia subacida
Phellinus pini
Postia sericeomollis
Stereum sanguinolentum
Veluticeps fimbriata

Sap Rots
Cryptoporus volvatus
Gleophyllum sepiarium
Trichaptum abietinum,

Canker Diseases
Atropellis piniphila

Conifer Rust Diseases
Stem and Broom
Cronartium coleosporioides
Cronartium comandrae
Cronartium comptoniae
Endocronartium harknessii
Needle
Melampsora albertensis
Melampsora occidentalis (inoculation only)

Conifer Needle Diseases
Davisomycella ampla
Elytroderma deformans
Herpotrichia juniperi
Lophodermella concolor
Lophodermium pinastri
Lophodermium seditiosum

Mycospaerella pini
Neopeckia coulteri

Dwarf Mistletoes
Arceuthobium americanum
Arceuthobium laricis (secondary host)
Arceuthobium tsugense (secondary host)

Ponderosa Pine
(***Pinus ponderosa*** Douglas ex P. Laws. & C. Laws.)

Root Diseases
Armillaria ostoyae
Armillaria sinapina
Heterobasidion annosum
Inonotus tomentosus
Leptographium wageneri
Phaeolus schweinitzii
Phellinus weirii

Heart Rots
Fomitopsis officinalis
Fomitopsis pinicola
Laetiporus sulphureus
Phellinus pini
Postia sericeomollis
Stereum sanguinolentum

Sap Rots
Cryptoporus volvatus
Gleopyllum sepiarium
Trichaptum abietinum

Canker Diseases
Atropellis piniphila

Conifer Rust Diseases
  Stem and Broom
Cronartium coleosporioides
Cronartium comandrae
Cronartium comptoniae
Endocronartium harknessii
  Needle
Melampsora albertensis
Melampsora occidentalis (inoculation only)

Conifer Needle Diseases
Elytroderma deformans
Lophodermella concolor

Lophodermium pinastri
Mycosphaerella pini

Dwarf Mistletoes
Arceuthobium americanum (secondary host)
Arceuthobium laricis (rare host)

Western White Pine
(***Pinus monticola*** Douglas *ex* D. Don)

Root Diseases
Armillaria ostoyae
Armillaria sinapina
Heterobasidion annosum
Inonotus tomentosus
Leptographium wageneri
Phaeolus schweinitzii
Phellinus weirii
Rhizina undulata

Heart Rots
Echinodontium tinctorium
Fomitopsis officinalis
Fomitopsis pinicola
Ganoderma applanatum
Laetiporus sulphureus
Perenniporia subacida
Phellinus pini
Postia sericeomollis
Stereum sanguinolentum

Sap Rots
Cryptoporus volvatus
Gleopyllum sepiarium
Trichaptum abietinum

Canker Diseases
Atropellis pinicola

Conifer Rust Diseases
  Stem and Broom
Cronartium ribicola
  Needle
Melampsora occidentalis (inoculation only)

Conifer Needle Diseases
Bifusella linearis
Herpotrichia juniperi
Mycosphaerella pini
Neopeckia coulteri

Dwarf Mistletoes
Arceuthobium laricis (rare host)
Arceuthobium tsugense (secondary host)

Spruce
Black Spruce
(***Picea mariana*** (Mill.) B. S. P.)

Root Diseases
Armillaria ostoyae
Armillaria sinapina
Inonotus tomentosus
Phaeolus schweinitzii

Heart Rots
Fomitopsis officinalis
Fomitopsis pinicola
Phellinus pini
Veluticeps fimbriata

Sap Rots
Cryptoporus volvatus
Gleopyllum sepiarium
Trichaptum abietinum

Conifer Rust Diseases
  Stem and Broom
Chrysomyxa arctostaphyli
Chrysomyxa ledicola
  Cone
Chrysomyxa pirolata

Conifer Needle Diseases
Lirula macrospora

Engelmann Spruce
(***Picea engelmannii*** Parry ex Engelm.)

Root Diseases
Armillaria ostoyae
Armillaria sinapina
Heterobasidion annosum
Inonotus tomentosus
Leptographium wageneri
Phaeolus schweinitzii
Phellinus weirii
Rhizina undulata

Heart Rots
Echinodontium tinctorium
Fomitopsis officinalis
Fomitopsis pinicola
Ganoderma applanatum
Hericium abietis
Laetiporus sulphureus
Perenniporia subacida
Phellinus pini
Postia sericeomollis
Stereum sanguinolentum
Veluticeps fimbriata

Sap Rots
Cryptoporus volvatus
Gleopyllum sepiarium
Trichaptum abietinum

Conifer Rust Diseases
  Stem and Broom
Chrysomyxa arctostaphyli
Chrysomyxa ledicola
  Cone
Chrysomyxa pirolata

Conifer Needle Diseases
Herpotrichia juniperi
Neopeckia coulteri
Lirula macrospora

Dwarf Mistletoes
Arceuthobium americanum (rare host)
Arceuthobium douglasii (rare host)
Arceuthobium laricis (rare host)
Arceuthobium tsugense (rare host)

White Spruce
(***Picea glauca*** Moench) Voss)

Root Diseases
Armillaria ostoyae
Armillaria sinapina
Heterobasidion annosum
Inonotus tomentosus
Leptographium wageneri
Phaeolus schweinitzii
Rhizina undulata

Heart Rots
Ceriporiopsis rivulosa
Echinodontium tinctorium
Fomitopsis officinalis
Fomitopsis pinicola
Ganoderma applanatum
Laetiporus sulphureus
Perenniporia subacida
Phellinus pini
Postia sericeomollis
Stereum sanguinolentum
Veluticeps fimbriata

Sap Rots
Cryptoporus volvatus
Gleopyllum sepiarium
Trichaptum abietinum

Conifer Rust Diseases
  Stem and Broom
Chrysomyxa arctostaphyli
Chrysomyxa ledicola
  Cone
Chrysomyxa pirolata

Conifer Needle Diseases
Herpotrichia juniperi
Lirula macrospora

Dwarf Mistletoes
Arceuthobium americanum (rare host)

Sitka Spruce
(**Picea sitchensis** Bong. Carrière)

Root Diseases
Armillaria ostoyae
Armillaria sinapina
Heterobasidion annosum
Inonotus tomentosus
Phaeolus schweinitzii
Phellinus weirii
Rhizina undulata

Heart Rots
Ceriporiopsis rivulosa
Echinodontium tinctorium
Fomitopsis officinalis
Fomitopsis pinicola

Ganoderma applanatum
Hericium abietis
Laetiporus sulphureus
Neolentinus kauffmanii
Perenniporia subacida
Phellinus pini
Postia sericeomollis
Stereum sanguinolentum
Veluticeps fimbriata

Sap Rots
Cryptoporus volvatus
Gleopyllum sepiarium
Trichaptum abietinum

Canker Diseases
Diaporthe lokoyae

Conifer Rust Diseases
  Stem and Broom
Chrysomyxa arctostaphyli
Chrysomyxa ledicola
  Cone
Chrysomyxa pirolata
Chrysomyxa monesis
  Needle
Melampsora albertensis (inoculation only)
Melampsora occidentalis (inoculation only)

Conifer Needle Diseases
Herpotrichia juniperi
Lirula macrospora

Dwarf Mistletoes
Arceuthobium tsugense (rare host)

True Fir
Subalpine Fir
(**Abies lasiocarpa** (Hook.) Nutt.)

Root Diseases
Armillaria ostoyae
Armillaria sinapina
Heterobasidion annosum
Inonotus tomentosus
Phaeolus schweinitzii
Phellinus weirii

Heart Rots
Echinodontium tinctorium

Fomitopsis pinicola
Ganoderma applanatum
Hericium abietis
Laetiporus sulphureus
Perenniporia subacida
Phellinus hartigii
Phellinus pini
Postia sericeomollis
Stereum sanguinolentum
Veluticeps fimbriata

Sap Rots
Chondrostereum purpureum
Cryptoporus volvatus
Gleopyllum sepiarium
Trichaptum abietinum

Conifer Rust Diseases
  Stem and Broom
Melampsorella caryophyllacearum
  Needle
Melampsora albertensis
Melampsora epitea
Melampsora abieti-capraearum
Pucciniastrum epilobii

Conifer Needle Diseases
Delphinella abietis
Delphinella balsameae
Herpotrichia juniperi

Dwarf Mistletoes
Arceuthobium laricis (rare host)
Arceuthobium tsugense (secondary host)

Amabilis Fir
(*Abies amabilis* Douglas ex Forbes)

Root Diseases
Armillaria ostoyae
Armillaria sinapina
Heterobasidion annosum
Inonotus tomentosus
Phaeolus schweinitzii
Phellinus weirii

Heart Rots
Ceriporiopsis rivulosa
Echinodontium tinctorium

Fomitopsis officinalis
Fomitopsis pinicola
Ganoderma applanatum
Hericium abietis
Laetiporus sulphureus
Perenniporia subacida
Phellinus hartigii
Phellinus pini
Stereum sanguinolentum
Veluticeps fimbriata

Sap Rots
Chondrostereum purpureum
Cryptoporus volvatus
Gleopyllum sepiarium
Trichaptum abietinum

Conifer Rust Diseases
  Stem and Broom
Melampsorella caryophyllacearum
  Needle
Melampsora epitea
Melampsora abieti-capraearum
Pucciniastrum epilobii

Conifer Needle Diseases
Herpotrichia juniperi

Dwarf Mistletoes
Arceuthobium tsugense (primary host)

Grand Fir (Balsam)
(*Abies grandis* (Douglas ex D. Don) Lindl.)

Root Diseases
Armillaria ostoyae
Armillaria sinapina
Heterobasidion annosum
Inonotus tomentosus
Leptographium wageneri
Phaeolus schweinitzii
Phellinus weirii (coast)
Rhizina undulata

Heart Rots
Ceriporiopsis rivulosa
Echinodontium tinctorium
Fomitopsis officinalis
Fomitopsis pinicola

Ganoderma applanatum
Hericium abietis
Laetiporus sulphureus
Perenniporia subacida
Phellinus pini
Postia sericeomollis
Stereum sanguinolentum
Veluticeps fimbriata

Sap Rots
Chondrostereum purpureum
Cryptoporus volvatus
Gleopyllum sepiarium
Trichaptum abietinum

Conifer Rust Diseases
  Stem and Broom
Melampsorella caryophyllacearum
  Needle
Melampsora albertensis (inoculation only)
Melampsora epitea
Melampsora abieti-capraearum
Pucciniastrum epilobii

Conifer Needle Diseases
Herpotrichia juniperi

Dwarf Mistletoes
Arceuthobium douglasii (rare host)
Arceuthobium laricis (rare host)
Arceuthobium tsugense (rare host)

Western Larch
(*Larix occidentalis* Nutt.)

Root Diseases
Armillaria ostoyae
Armillaria sinapina
Heterobasidion annosum
Inonotus tomentosus
Phaeolus schweinitzii
Phellinus weirii (interior)
Rhizina undulata

Heart Rots
Ceriporiopsis rivulosa
Echinodontium tinctorium
Fomitopsis officinalis
Fomitopsis pinicola
Laetiporus sulphureus

Perenniporia subacida
Phellinus pini
Postia sericeomollis
Stereum sanguinolentum
Veluticeps fimbriata

Sap Rots
Cryptoporus volvatus
Gleopyllum sepiarium
Trichaptum abietinum

Canker Diseases
Diaporthe lokoyae

Conifer Rust Diseases
  Needle
Melampsora albertensis
Melampsora epitea
Melampsora paradoxa
Melampsora occidentalis (inoculation only)

Conifer Needle Diseases
Hypodermella laricis
Meria laricis

Dwarf Mistletoes
Arceuthobium laricis (primary host)

Western Redcedar
(*Thuja plicata* Donn *ex* D. Don)

Root Diseases
Armillaria ostoyae
Armillaria sinapina
Heterobasidion annosum
Inonotus tomentosus
Phaeolus schweinitzii
Phellinus weirii (cedar form - interior)
Rhizina undulata

Heart Rots
Ceriporiopsis rivulosa
Fomitopsis pinicola
Ganoderma applanatum
Laetiporus sulphureus
Perenniporia subacida (coast)
Phellinus pini
Postia sericeomollis
Stereum sanguinolentum
Veluticeps fimbriata

Sap Rots
Chondrostereum purpureum
Gleopyllum sepiarium
Trichaptum abietinum

Canker Diseases
Diaporthe lokoyae

Conifer Needle Diseases
Didymascella thujina
Herpotrichia juniperi

Yellow cedar
(***Chamaecyparis nootkaensis*** (D. Don) Spach)

Root Diseases
Armillaria ostoyae
Armillaria sinapina
Phellinus weirii (cedar form)

Heart Rots
Fomitopsis pinicola
Phellinus pini
Postia sericeomollis

Sap Rots

Gleopyllum sepiarium

Conifer Needle Diseases
Herpotrichia juniperi

Selected Disease Organisms Grouped by Common Signs or Symptoms

Samples of diseased material often have distinct characteristics that can help identify or at least narrow down the list of causal organisms. The following lists are presented as an aid to identification based on commonly observed, easily recognizable signs and symptoms.

Brown cubical decay

Cryptoporus volvatus
Fomitopsis officinalis
Fomitopsis pinicola
Gleophyllum sepiarium
Laetiporus sulphureus
Neolentinus kauffmanii
Phaeolus schweinitzii
Piptoporus betulinus
Postia sericeomollis

Laminated decay

Ceriporiopsis rivulosa
Echinodontium tinctorium
Perenniporia subacida
Phellinus weirii
Pholiota populnea
Spongipellis delectans

White pocket rot

Hericium abietis
Heterobasidion annosum
Inonotus tomentosus
Perenniporia subacida
Phellinus pini
Trichaptum abietinum

Mycelial mats

Armillaria spp.
Fomes fomentarius
Fomitopsis officinalis
Fomitopsis pinicola
Gleophyllum sepiarium
Laetiporus sulphureus
Perenniporia subacida
Piptoporus betulinus
Postia sericeomollis
Stereum sanguinolentum

Stringy decay

Armillaria spp.
Echinodontium tinctorium
Hericium abietis
Heterobasidion annosum
Spongipellis delectans

Soft or spongy decay

Armillaria spp.
Fomes fomentarius
Ganoderma applanatum
Heterobasidion annosum
Inonotus obliquus
Perenniporia subacida
Phellinus igniarius
Phellinus tremulae
Trichaptum abietinum
Veluticeps fimbriata

General Index

—C—

—F—

—G—

—H—